The French Huguenots
and Wars of Religion

The French Huguenots and Wars of Religion

Three Centuries of Resistance for Freedom of Conscience

STEPHEN M. DAVIS

Foreword by William Edgar

WIPF & STOCK · Eugene, Oregon

THE FRENCH HUGUENOTS AND WARS OF RELIGION
Three Centuries of Resistance for Freedom of Conscience

Wipf & Stock
An Imprint of Wipf and Stock Publishers
199 W. 8th Ave., Suite 3
Eugene, OR 97401

www.wipfandstock.com

PAPERBACK ISBN: 978-1-5326-6161-7
HARDCOVER ISBN: 978-1-5326-6162-4
EBOOK ISBN: 978-1-5326-6163-1

OCTOBER 19, 2021

Contents

Foreword

The Truth of the Huguenots

MOST PEOPLE CURSORILY ACQUAINTED with the French Huguenots are likely familiar with a few highlights. They know about notorious incidents such as the Saint Bartholomew's Day massacre (Aug 24, 1572). Many will be aware of the refuge in various countries, particularly if they claim Huguenot ancestry. But few will have made the connection between the Huguenot diaspora and a number of characteristic modern issues. Yet there is much to learn here. In part because of the Huguenot displacement, Europe was split into a Protestant North and a Roman Catholic South, a geopolitical difference still affecting our modern world. But many significant questions attend to this history worth looking at closely today. There are admittedly significant differences between Huguenot history and modern concerns, but also important parallels between the post-Reformation world and today that should concern us.

I wish to highlight three areas of concern. First, facing persecution. To be a Protestant in sixteenth to eighteenth century France was often to be an oppressed minority. Their attitude before their oppressors is inspiring. Second, what should be our policies regarding the sending countries? Oftentimes the reasons for refugees fleeing from their motherland reveal serious unresolved problems at home. And third, how should the receiving countries welcome and integrate immigrants? Not only in the United States, but in many European countries there is considerable ambiguity about how to amalgamate refugees without dishonoring their culture.

PERSECUTION

Generally, historians of the Huguenots distinguish between the first refuge, and the second or the great refuge. The first refuge is usually dated between 1560 and 1585, although persecutions certainly began earlier. John Calvin was himself in effect a refugee to the city of Geneva, which city received thousands of Huguenots over the years. He ministered to the persecuted Protestants still in France as well. One of the most moving examples of this was his communications to the five young men of Lyon. The story has often been told.[1] In 1552 five young graduates from the Seminary in Lausanne were headed back to France in order to lead the churches there. But they were trapped and detained in Lyon. Calvin wrote letters of encouragement to the young men. But he also wrote several authorities to plead for their release. And he encouraged visitors to come and support them, even though it might be costly to do so. In the end, though, the five men were executed. While they were alive, Calvin's message to them was one of commending patience, and ultimately taking refuge in the knowledge of God's good providence. "It cannot be but that you feel some twinges of frailty; yet, be confident that he whose service you are upon will so rule in your hearts by his Holy Spirit, that his grace shall overcome all temptations… You must therefore keep this sentence in mind, that *he who dwells in you is stronger than the world.*"

There is much to learn from Calvin's concern for the persecuted Huguenots. Today, the number of Christians threatened in their faith is astonishing. Organizations such as Open Doors show fifty countries where Christians face severe persecution. Some three hundred forty million believers are in constant danger, one in eight persons. Just to focus on one example among many: Myanmar, which is often in the news, is a place where it is hard to be a Christian. Out of a population of some fifty-five million, over four million are followers of Christ. There are a number of Bible schools and seminaries in the country, most of them illegal. Persecution comes from the Buddhists, supported by the government through the military. A number of Christian organizations are at work encouraging perseverance in the faith. One of the most effective is the Institute for Global Engagement. Unlike some groups which are not sensitive to the local context, the IGE penetrates at the request of locals, building up trust and credibility. For

---

1. A moving account is by Derek Thomas, https://www.desiringgod.org/articles/adieu -adieu-my-brother.

example, in partnership with the Kachin Baptist Convention, they sponsor seminars and discipleship groups for the largely Christian Kachin people group. Like Calvin, they appeal to the authorities as they seek to help believers navigate the oppressive laws of the country.

ORIGINATING COUNTRIES

Persecutions take root when the homeland cannot deal satisfactorily with its dissidents. It may seem disingenuous to take issue with the city of Geneva's insufficiencies, since it was a model of welcoming refugees. But it was not only a receiving place, but a sending place. Upon their arrival Huguenots were put into the city registry as "inhabitants" giving them a more permanent status than visitors, but yet with no political rights. To be registered they had to subscribe to a written statement assuring that they were there *seulement pour le désir qu'il a de vivre selon la sainte religion évangélique ici purement annoncée* ("only for his desire to live according to the holy evangelical religion purely practiced here").[2] Not only were they second class citizens but only welcomed upon this strict Protestant confession.

The most problematic sending country was of course France itself. France from the sixteenth century onward has never been able to assign a proper place for the Huguenots. Despite the Revolutionary slogan, Liberty, Equality, Fraternity, Protestants have never quite enjoyed genuine equality with the rest of the population. It is true that in the decades after the Reign of Terror (1793) Protestants have found themselves occupying places of influence beyond what their population would suggest. Yet in the country's attempt to enforce *laïcité*, the French equivalent of secularization, evangelicals have been considered a sect (a cult) at least until recognized scholars such as the Baptist Sébastien Fath published articles in the influential newspaper *Le Monde* proving that evangelicals were part of the historic Christian tradition.[3] His arguments are reminiscent of Calvin's *Preface to François 1er* where he informs the king that Protestantism was a successor to the historic Christian faith.

In a somewhat dated, but nevertheless still powerful essay, *Le mal français*, the prominent Minister of Justice Alain Peyrefitte argued that France had lost its effectiveness in business and as a world broker. The reason was

2. See https://www.huguenotsociety.org/geneva-the-protestants-rome/.

3. See https://evangelicalfocus.com/culture/1761/protestantism-and-media-in-france-el-monde-sebastian-fath.

centralization and bureaucracy. Her original sin was to have persecuted the Huguenots! Perhaps a bit idealistically, he praised the Huguenots for their spirit of industry and creativity and considered France's exclusion of them a sort of national suicide. In a way, this was the same kind of error committed by Germany when it persecuted the Jews. In addition to being an unspeakable evil, it drained the country of some of its best minds, including Albert Einstein and many others. This had the unintended consequence of strengthening the countries of refuge, be they enemies or the oppressors. It was the same for the Huguenots, who enriched the countries that harbored them.

Here is a call to address the root causes of exile. What would France have looked like had she developed a proper pluralism and the promotion of freedom achieved by her neighbors? Today we are facing the greatest number of displaced persons in history. With that has come the nearly intractable problem of immigration policy. As of today, some two hundred seventy-two million people migrate from their home country. That is close to 4 percent of the world's population. Interestingly, India is the main origin of international migrants, and Mexico and China are close behind. The United States and parts of Western Europe are among the largest destinations. The chief causes for people leaving their homelands include looking for work, escaping conflict, and climate.

While many countries have been fairly generous in receiving refugees, it is clear that the trend cannot be open-ended. Perhaps far too slowly, it has occurred to them to look more closely at the originating countries to see if their local problems could not be addressed. The problem is that they are fraught with corruption and drug trafficking. The U.S. shares some of the blame, since it needs low-wage workers and often sends confusing messages about who is welcome and who is not. There are enormous issues attending to this kind of initiative. Food shortages, cocaine smuggling, uneven use of U. S. moneys, humanitarian exploitation, but they must be faced.

RECEIVING COUNTRIES

Finally, those countries on the welcoming end of displaced persons need to work out a viable policy of integration. The Huguenots fled to places such as Holland, Great Britain, Germany and the United States. Often, but not always, they were welcomed with compassion for their plight. Occasionally, though, jealousies emerged and even marginalization. In general, the

Huguenots came from the same cultural backgrounds as their hosts. Today, by contrast, immigrants and displaced persons may come from radically different backgrounds. The obvious case in point is Muslims, who bring with them convictions and practices which are in sharp contrast to those of the receiving countries.

One difficult, but practical step to take is to engage with the sending countries and anticipate problems before the refugees come to our borders. This requires skillfully exercised diplomacy. Pope Francis has made it a regular theme in his public campaigns to plead for the creation of more jobs in the sending countries which should obviate the desperate need to immigrate. It is also the key to promoting human dignity.[4]

The United States has also turned its attention to resolving problems in those countries from which refugees are leaving. Vice President Kamala Harris has been tasked to visit the "Northern Triangle" countries, Guatemala, El Salvador and Honduras, with the goal of helping to eradicate the drug traffickers which are often the perpetrators of the terrorism that forces people to flee.[5] Of course, this is far from a simple task. But it makes sense in the light of the refugee crisis. And the receiving countries must find a reasonable way to integrate the immigrants. Determining the numbers is an enormous challenge. The Genevans struggled to find the balance. They erred on the side of generosity.

But the deeper problem is finding a way to live together in an atmosphere of freedom and justice, with people coming from vastly different horizons. There is no simple answer to this. Had we followed Alain Peyrefitte's instincts there would be a wise way to arrive at principled pluralism. The full defense of this position is somewhat involved. The most convincing version of it can be called *Covenantal Pluralism*. This approach's most persuasive defense is by the trio, W. Christopher Stewart, Chris Seiple & Dennis R. Hoover.[6] They argue that genuine pluralism is far removed from *tolerance*, which is paternalistic at best, and relativist at worst.

4. See https://www.catholicsun.org/2014/03/22/job-creation-is-essential-for-promoting-human-dignity-pope-says/.

5. See https://www.nbcnews.com/news/latino/central-america-drying-farmers-face-choice-pray-rain-or-leave-n1027346.

6. See their article, "Toward a Global Covenant of Peaceable Neighborhood: Introducing the Philosophy of Covenantal Pluralism," in *The Review of Faith and International Affairs* vol 18, 2020, https://www.tandfonline.com/doi/full/10.1080/15570274.2020.183 5029.

Instead, true pluralism must recognize the deeply held convictions of those with whom we differ. This can be most uncomfortable. But it demands mutual trust and a willingness to "love thy neighbor" even though that requires sitting at the feet of his culture. But doesn't this require some kind of common bond, a level playing field? Covenantal pluralism depends on shared underlying principles. As our authors put it, "However, some key commonalities across most of these pluralisms are that they eschew simplistic relativism, approach the challenges of diversity with realism but not fatalism, and envision a positive pluralism that calls not for mere side-by-side, arms-length coexistence but for a principled engagement across religious and worldview divides."

While we want to avoid a kind of top-down state-controlled doctrine, there must be minimal agreement about the rules of coexistence. "Covenantal" suggests trust, respect, even freedom, which are not abstract ideas but are rooted in a biblical notion of justice and mutual respect. Without such a basis, we will devolve into anything but true pluralism.

Those are some of the lessons we learn from the Huguenots. May we emulate their achievements and apply their insights into today's world. The book you are about to read will help discover them.

William Edgar,
Professor of apologetics at Westminster Theological Seminary,
associate professor at the Faculté Jean Calvin,
former President of the Huguenot Fellowship.

Preface

IN 2017 MY WIFE and I visited the Tower of Constance in Aigues-Mortes in the south of France. It was a sobering experience to ponder the suffering of Huguenot women who had been imprisoned in the stark, cold tower, some for decades. Although I had heard of the Huguenots, I had little knowledge of their history, their suffering, and their contribution to the concepts of freedom of conscience and worship. Perhaps Marie Durand, whose family endured countless hardships, is the most well-known Huguenot prisoner. Her mother was arrested at a covert worship gathering and died in prison. Her brother Pierre, a Protestant pastor, was arrested and executed. Her father, likewise, was imprisoned for his faith. Marie married Mathieu Serre who was arrested after their secret marriage. In 1730 Marie was arrested at the age of eighteen and imprisoned in the Tower of Constance for thirty-eight years until her release in 1768. There is an inscription engraved in stone in the Tower of Constance—"*Résistez*." It is not known if Marie wrote this. In any case, she remains a symbol of steadfast faith and of resistance to religious intolerance in the centuries-long struggle for the freedom of conscience. We are reminded that in our day religious freedom is still under attack from those who want to impose either state control, a state church, or unbelief.

There is much to learn from our spiritual ancestors, the Huguenots. They live on today, not only in the memory and practices of their spiritual descendants, but in the benefits of their combat which have accrued to others who desire to worship freely without state, religious or anti-religious interference. We are in their debt. We might also follow in their train as religious freedoms are increasingly undermined and believers are pushed to the margins of society as outlaws. May we have Huguenot conviction and courage to remain faithful, and to not be ashamed of our heavenly calling! May we have the courage to deny the impulse to control the hearts and minds of others, or to deny for others what we want for ourselves—FREEDOM!

Introduction

JACQUES BARZUN, IN HIS book, *From Dawn to Decadence: 1500 to the Present*, covers five centuries of western civilization. His monumental tome sketches the development of the West's cultural life. Although my writing does not hold a candle to Barzun's, I take some small comfort in believing that my book can cover a mere three centuries. In consulting Barzun's extensive index, I discovered six pages with reference to the Huguenots and over a dozen entries on hygiene. In my book there are no references to hygiene but I hope to provide more insight into Huguenot history and the Wars of Religion.

The term "Wars of Religion" is often used technically for a particular sixteenth-century period (1562–1598).[1] By most accounts there were eight wars or conflicts during this period. There is room to question whether there were eight wars or really one war with intermittent periods of truce and broken treaties. Mack Holt expands this period in *The French Wars of Religion, 1562–1629* and includes early seventeenth-century conflicts following the 1598 Edict of Nantes. He understands the Edict of Nantes more in line with previous edicts of pacification as a temporary measure with Henri IV's intention to reestablish Catholic unity in the kingdom rather than a desire to institute a policy of genuine tolerance. In covering an even longer period for the Wars of Religion, I have followed French historians Pierre Miquel in *Les guerres de religion* (1980) and Raoul Stéphan in *L'Épopée huguenote* (1943) who include the War of the Camisards in the early 1700s and persecutions preceding the Edict of Tolerance in 1787 which granted Protestants full civil status and freedom of conscience. They

---

1. Benedict, "Wars of Religion, 1562–1598," 147–75.

also provide eyewitness testimony from sources rarely found in English-language books on the Huguenots.[2]

According to Stéphan, the term "Protestant" was not employed widely in France until the seventeenth century and non-Lutheran, Reformed believers were called Huguenots.[3] Among historians, the origin and first usage of the term "Huguenot" have been widely debated with little consensus. Some believe that the term "Huguenot" derives from the "Swiss-German word for 'confederate,' *Eidgnoss*," and the "term *eiguenot* or *eyguenot* represents the Genevan attempt to reproduce the term for 'confederate.'"[4] Historians of the sixteenth century generally held that the name first emerged during the conspiracy of Amboise in 1560 to kidnap François II, possibly a term of derision invented by the house of Guise to designate Huguenots as the descendants of Hugues Capet. There are testimonies of its use in different localities before that date but they appear inconclusive.[5] A seventeenth-century historian noted that Huguenot, as other words, often entered into universal usage without knowing the origin or occasion. In any case, he asserts that the term was not considered an insult.[6] A novel alternative comes from French pastor Charles Bost who has written extensively on the subject of French Protestantism. He believes that the name originated from the Huguenot practice of meeting secretly at night and the accusations against the Huguenots of various vices. In this interpretation, an evil mythical spirit, King Hugon wandered at night and his name became attached to the Huguenots (*les petits loups-garous*), that is, werewolves.[7] In any case, Carter Lindberg states that "the French Calvinists preferred the term *Réformés*, the Reformed. Catholic satires of the time called them *la Religion Déformée*."[8] After the Revocation of the Edict of Nantes under Louis XIV, the banned religion became officially designated R.P.R, *religion prétendue réformée* (so-called reformed religion) in order to exclude churches from society which were rooted in the Protestant Reformation.[9]

---

2. All translations are my own.

3. Stéphan, *L'Épopée huguenote*, 65.

4. McGrath, *Life of John Calvin*, 88.

5. "Peut-on préciser?" 122–23.

6. Benoist, *Histoire de l'édit de Nantes*, 401–2.

7. Bost, *Histoire des Protestants*, 58–59.

8. Lindberg, *European Reformation*, 282.

9. Carbonnier-Burkard, *La révolte des Camisards*, 9.

My modest aim in this book is to highlight some of the major person-
ages and events surrounding three centuries of violence and resistance in
French Huguenot history. I cannot count the blank stares or tortured expla-
nations I have received from people at the mention of the word "Huguenot,"
which led me to imagine the book more as a primer than a scholarly tome.
For those who seek to know more about French kings, European wars, Reformers, Huguenot emigration to places of refuge, and the almost infinite
details of life, occupations, plagues, and religious controversy, there are
many books suited for those purposes. For example, Barbara Diefendorf's
excellent book *Beneath the Cross: Catholics and Huguenots in Sixteenth-
Century Paris* treats in great detail the period of early religious violence
from 1557 to the Saint Bartholomew's Day massacre in 1572. G. R. Elton's
Reformation Europe covers the period from 1517 to 1559 and Roland H.
Bainton's *The Reformation of the Sixteenth Century* provides a thorough
treatment of the starting point and foundation of the remarkable history of
the Huguenots. Of the many books on the Reformers, Alister E. McGrath's
A Life of John Calvin and *Luther's Theology of the Cross* are good resources
along with Olivier Christin's *Les Réformes: Luther, Calvin et les protestants.*
In my focus on the Huguenots and their struggles, I have purposely limited
myself to the fine thread of their cause for freedom of conscience and have
consciously chosen breadth over depth in trying to cover a period spanning
three centuries. In so doing, my work is selective, more narrative than ana-
lytical, in recounting the political and religious factors which contributed
to the Wars of Religion and finally led to religious freedom for Protestants.
Although this book is primarily intended as an accessible introduction for
those unacquainted with Huguenot history, students and teachers of history might find some benefit as I draw from French-language sources not
found in other books on the subject. Other European nations and events
are included but mostly in connection with my narrow emphasis on France.
The bibliography at the end of the book will provide help to those who want
to go deeper into the minutiae of European history from gifted authors who
specialize in those areas.

Any discussion of religious history cannot be completely dispassion-
ate or impartial. Unbiased historians do not exist, and Barzun, while as-
serting the possibility of some measure of objectivity, considers it a "waste
of breath to point out that every observer is in some way biased."[10] This
is doubly true when speaking of Wars of Religion. Or were they political

10. Barzun, *From Dawn to Decadence*, x.

wars, or both? There are cautions to take in attempting to write about the Huguenots and their combat for religious freedom. We need to consider the immense complexity of the origins of the Reformation and the failure of Protestantism to win the day against the established Church in France. We also need to understand the contradiction of testimonies to the events and the recording of these testimonies. The Huguenots have been demonized by some, mythologized by others. While we realize these limitations we can still try to understand what took place during centuries of struggle for people who simply wanted to worship unmolested by a dominant and oppressive religion which acted in concert with an increasingly absolute monarchism.

Although I had no intention of writing a hagiography, I did discover that certain events, exact dates, or the ascription of fault are open to dispute and I might be faulted for my recounting of certain events. Historians do not write with one voice. Both Protestants and Catholic historians might fall prey to selectivity in their attempt to cast others in the worst possible light and might be embarrassed to admit responsibility for religious violence. Martin asserts that most Protestant historians, when discussing events in France, are inclined "to give a hostile interpretation to documents relating to the papacy and its agents."[11] Diefendorf talks about "a long historiographical tradition that has tended to see the Wars of Religion—in spite of their name—as having been shaped more by political than by religious motivations."[12] McGrath concurs that the Wars of Religion "were first and foremost wars which centered on religious issues—above all, the agenda laid down in Geneva by John Calvin."[13] There were certainly excesses of zeal and retaliation by the oppressed against their oppressors. There were times that the cup of sorrows they drank led to revenge and retaliation against their enemies. Also, many identified with the Huguenot cause for different motives without a grasp of Reformation teachings and without evidence of gospel transformation in their lives. That is, they were Huguenot in name only. There were others who vacillated between Catholicism and Protestantism for political gain according to the prevailing partisan winds or were induced to convert for monetary gain. There were peasants who sought to escape the crushing taxes paid to the Church or feigned conversion out of fear of fines, imprisonment, kidnapping of their children, or confiscation

11. Martin, "Papal Policy," 38–39.

12. Diefendorf, *Beneath the Cross*, 5.

13. McGrath, *Life of John Calvin*, 193.

of their possessions. Others who were genuine followers of Christ and had embraced the doctrine of the Reformed tradition did not always live and behave in a manner consistent with the gospel. Yet we must remember their context. The Huguenots frequently swore unfeigned loyalty to the French crown and petitioned kings for their rights. Yet they were systematically attacked as traitors. Their petitions were mostly ignored and their loyalty questioned because they did not profess the religion of the king. State-sanctioned religion refused to accept as full citizens those whose ultimate allegiance could never be offered to fallible human leaders, religious or secular.

Different and biased perspectives on the Huguenots should not prevent us from looking at history and learning from the errors which have a way of repeating themselves in our day. My purpose is not to present a Protestant or Catholic perspective although my evangelical sensibilities will become readily apparent. As G. R. Elton quipped, "If I cannot hope to have pleased all sides, I can at least suppose that I have in different places displeased them all equally."[14] The hostility between two religious confessions is no longer the burning issue in most of the West. Until recent times, the evolution of the State and the modern notion of separation of Church and State had brought about an uneasy truce or grudging accommodation in most pluralistic nations. Current events in France and other Western nations indicate a change in mood toward religion, increased hostility toward those who refuse to accept state dictates which contradict traditional and biblical positions on morality, and a further push of religious beliefs to the margins of society. Never for one moment should we naively believe that either spiritual or civil authorities can be accorded blind trust to defend the rights which were granted by God and gained by the shedding of martyrs' blood. The freedom of conscience, the freedom to believe or not believe, the freedom to worship or the freedom to refuse to worship, or worship differently, are fundamental freedoms granted by God which the State and the Church must recognize. We must denounce the tyranny of any State in a drift to totalitarianism and likewise deplore the drift of any religion or irreligion toward intolerance, repression, and the binding of consciences.

From Jean Vallière, burned at the stake in 1523 and designated by many as the first Protestant martyr, to Pastor Charmuzy toward the end of the eighteenth century, imprisoned for nine days before dying from vicious beatings, there were three centuries of confrontations between the Catholic and Reformed religions leading to thousands of victims on both

14. Elton, *Reformation Europe*, xi.

sides throughout France. The slow combat of the Huguenots for religious freedom and the long struggle of Catholics for the reform of the Church touched most French people with their savage flames beginning with the sixteenth century. The ideas of Luther and Calvin brought not only war and torture but ushered France into the modern world, a world where each one may freely choose and passionately defend his or her religion or irreligion, and where no one should risk losing their lives for belief or unbelief through intolerance or coercion. This story of the Huguenots is also our story in the measure in which we live out the principles they defended and for which many gave their lives.

This book mostly treats French Protestantism of the Reformed faith without neglecting the immense influence of Luther in France in the early sixteenth century and the shared history of Lutheran and Reformed Christians in their common struggle for religious freedom. Protestant Lutheranism originated with the arrival of Luther's writings into France and began to take root before Calvin appeared on the scene. Such was Luther's influence that many early heretics were called "Lutheran" as a term of derision. They had little knowledge of Luther or his writings and later Huguenots were sometimes referred to as Lutherans. After years of trouble and with a desire for peace, the Diet of Augsburg convened in 1555. The peace of Augsburg in 1555 lasted sixty-three years, ended conflict between Catholics and Lutherans in Germany and recognized the freedom of worship wherever princes and municipal authorities professed the Lutheran faith.[15] Almost a century later, Swiss troops liberated Alsace in 1632 from Catholic control and restored Protestantism until 1681when Strasbourg capitulated to France. Catholic churches were reopened alongside Lutheran churches. After the Revocation of the Edict of Nantes in 1685, Louis XIV (1638–1715) sought to reintroduce Catholicism to the region but without the open persecution practiced elsewhere. One of the king's measures to convert Lutherans was the practice, known as the *simultaneum*, of Lutheran and Catholic churches worshipping in the same edifices.[16]

The provinces of today's eastern France in Alsace were in the German orbit in the sixteenth century and had closer contact with Luther's native country. Until the Revolution those of the Reformed faith were tolerated by Lutheran authorities in eastern provinces. At the Revolution, these Reformed churches received the same legal status as churches of

15. Elton, *Reformation Europe*, 188.
16. Bost, *Histoire des Protestants*, 239–41.

their confession in the rest of France with the Edict of Toleration in 1787.[17] It is Elton's opinion that "Calvin's more drastic views quickly replaced a Lutheranism that might have been able to work with the crown" but the crucial reason for the lack of success of Lutheranism outside of Germany in France and elsewhere was that "the Reformation failed to win the support of princes and magistrates."[18]

If after reading the preceding paragraphs you decide to continue reading, allow me to direct your attention to the book's development. In the first chapter, I begin with an examination of the state of the Church[19] and political turmoil in the sixteenth century to understand how the religious and political soil had been prepared for the Reformation. Chapter 2 introduces several of the most influential Reformers and their motivations for reform. Chapter 3 treats the emergence of repression and persecution in response to spreading Reformation teaching during the first half of the sixteenth century. This includes the failed attempts of reform within the Church in the city of Meaux. Chapter 4 describes events which preceded the eight Wars of Religion and made the wars inevitable. Chapter 5 traces these eight wars from 1562 to 1598 which ended with the Edict of Nantes under Henri IV, Huguenot turned Catholic, a watershed edict which granted a measure of tolerance for Protestants. Chapters 6 and 7 look at the provisions of the Edict of Nantes and restrictions placed on Protestants, the Revocation of the Edict of Nantes under Louis XIV in 1685, and the War of the Camisards in the Cévennes region of France. Chapter 8 brings us to the French Revolution where the tables were turned against the Church and the Monarchy, when Protestants finally were recognized as fully French, and to the principle of freedom of conscience announced in the Declaration of the Rights of Man and of the Citizen. The short-lived Revolution did not live up to all of its ideals. Soon after there were reversals under Napoleon Bonaparte and the monarchy was reestablished. The struggles and state interference continued but the religious wars ended. The conclusion reminds us that the hard-won struggles for religious freedom are under attack in the twenty-first century. The actors and scenes have changed. The combat continues for the freedom to worship without coercion, fear of repression, or government surveillance. Believers, whose consciences are bound by the Word of God, and who are called to respect the established orders, might still pay

17. Bost, *Histoire des Protestants*, 244.
18. Elton, *Reformation Europe*, 83.
19. Unless otherwise indicated, "Church" refers to the Roman Catholic Church.

a price for their refusal to swear ultimate allegiance to Caesar, when they must obey God rather than man.

Chapter 1

Shattered Dream of Christian Unity

AT THE DAWN OF the sixteenth century, there were elements in place to fracture the coercive unity of the Christian religion in France and challenge the growing absolutism of the monarchy. For centuries Europe had endured disaster after disaster and the Catholic Church had experienced division and contestations to her authority. The Black Plague from 1346 to 1353 had taken over twenty-five million lives; the Hundred Years' War finally ended in 1453; and Constantinople was captured by the Ottoman Turks that same year. Haunted by death and the prospect of final judgment, people turned to the Church and to her saints for protection. The dogma of purgatory was promulgated as an intermediate place between heaven and hell and led the Church to offer indulgences to shorten the period of suffering. The sale of indulgences by the Dominican monk Johann Tetzel in Germany provoked Luther's ire and led to his protest in posting Ninety-Five Theses on the door of the Castle Church in Wittenberg on October 31, 1517. He had seen the corruption of the Church firsthand during a visit to Rome, and his eyes were soon opened to the wondrous biblical and apostolic truth of justification by faith. As a faithful Catholic monk, Luther initially sought the reform of the Church from within. In time he would understand the Church's intransigence and the impossibility of significant reform.[1]

1. Bost, *Histoire des Protestants*, 28.

STATE OF THE CHURCH

Prior to the Reformation, the monarchy and the Church in France were wedded without religious competition. The Church communicated to the faithful only fragments of Scripture interpreted by the Church and in Latin which the common people did not understand, and belief in the Church had replaced belief in the gospel of Jesus Christ. The pope claimed to represent Jesus Christ as the Vicar of Christ on earth, and the decrees of popes were placed on the same level of authority as Holy Scripture. Rather than accepting criticism or attempting reformation, the Church condemned and silenced her critics.[2] The religious and political foment of the sixteenth century challenged the status quo and brought significant changes. The emergence of a religious minority in a kingdom of Catholic religion and culture led to confessional and political confrontation.[3] Kelley states that "within a generation the ostensibly religious upheaval precipitated by Luther involved not only the formal break-up of Christendom but a whole range of secular disturbances."[4] Scholars uniformly look to the Reformation as the beginning of religious, social, and political turmoil in France which would destabilize both the monarchy and the Church. In a few decades, the Reformation's influence in France "not only shattered the unity of religion, but it led to the contesting of the monarchy itself."[5] This new religion became known as Calvinism and its followers were called Huguenots.[6]

The Catholic Church had been in decline for centuries, and long before the Reformation "the disintegration of this stupendous structure of theocracy and theology had already set in."[7] Bainton asserts that "the four hundred years preceding the Reformation had been characterized not only by the disintegration of the papal power . . . but also by the rise of sectarian movements splitting off from the Church."[8] There was a widespread spiritual crisis throughout Europe with multiple causes. Some have pointed to the Church's accumulation of wealth and territory, widespread corruption, or to the increasing power of the papacy. Above all, at the root of the spiritual

2. Bost, *Histoire des Protestants*, 17–18.

3. Garrisson, *Histoire des protestants*, 11.

4. Kelley, *Beginning of Ideology*, 7.

5. Holt, "Kingdom of France," 23.

6. Carbonnier-Burkard, *La révolte des Camisards*, 13.

7. Bainton, *Reformation of the Sixteenth Century*, 12.

8. Bainton, *Reformation of the Sixteenth Century*, 18.

crisis was the Church's "total inability to bring peace and solace to troubled generations in an era of dissolving certainties . . . . The consolations of the Church failed to satisfy."[9] There were also attempts at reform from within the Catholic Church which targeted the clergy and religious life. Those who called for reform denounced the abuses of the clergy at all levels of the hierarchical ladder, from the absentee bishops accumulating undeserved privileges, to the ignorant and concubinary village priests, and to the lazy and drunken monks. The Council of Trent (1545–1563) would mount a Counter-Reformation to the Protestant Reformation to establish Catholic dogma and attempt a reform of the pervasive moral laxity and indiscipline among the clergy.[10] Historians are not in agreement on whether to call these attempts at reform from within the Counter-Reformation or Catholic Reform. They do largely concur "that there were traditions of protest and renewal that went back well into the fifteenth century and in themselves owed nothing to the Protestant revolution."[11]

Although the Church throughout Europe was similar in "corruption, worldliness, spiritual lassitude, immorality, and uselessness," nations of Europe experienced the Reformation and responded in different ways.[12] A greater penetration of reform took place in Germany than in France. In France, at least initially, the Reformation made great inroads. Followers of Erasmus like Lefèvre d'Étaples (1455–1536) sought reform from within the Church to address the shocking state of affairs. They recognized that many priests were notoriously uneducated, that the high clergy lived in luxury at the expense of the beleaguered faithful, and many monasteries experienced a lack of discipline and a decline in morals. They were scandalized by the sale of indulgences which were solicited to finance the construction of the Basilica of Saint Peter in Rome. These early attempts at reform were ultimately unsuccessful, their advocates soon identified as Lutherans, and they were swiftly condemned as traitors to the State and heretics in the eyes of the Church.[13]

---

9. Elton, *Reformation Europe*, 11.

10. Baubérot and Carbonnier-Burkard, *Histoire des Protestants*, 16.

11. Elton, *Reformation Europe*, 125.

12. Elton, *Reformation Europe*, 68.

13. Elton, *Reformation Europe*, 75.

DISTURBANCE OF RELIGIOUS UNITY

The Church in Western Europe during the Middle Ages experienced a fragile unity as people sought refuge from their earthly fears and superstitions,
and consolation for the afterlife. There were schisms, notably that of the
Eastern Church in the eleventh century, and competing popes with rival
claims for the papal throne during the fourteenth century produced a crisis of authority and damaged the Church's prestige. The Church remained
powerful, visible with her grand cathedrals, impressive in her pageantry,
and holding authoritative sway over consciences with council decrees and
papal bulls. Through the relentless and iniquitous efforts of the Inquisition,
those sects considered the most dangerous, the Cathars and Albigensians,
largely disappeared by the fourteenth century. The Waldensians (*Vaudois*)
survived, were given new momentum, and suffered further persecution
during the sixteenth-century Reformation.[14] The Inquisition raged for
centuries and became a powerful tool of the Church to combat Protestant
heretics in the sixteenth century. The Church determined what to think
and what to reject. Individuals did not have the right or capacity to think
for themselves, and personal choices were considered heresy. Throughout
Europe, there were breaches made in this coercive unity of thought. Arab
versions of Aristotle's writings began to circulate in Latin during the Middle
Ages. Dissonant European voices arose—Abelard (1079–1141), precursor
of Descartes and scientific doubt; Roger Bacon (1220–1292), who spent
most of his life in prison; John Hus (1369–1415), burned at the stake at the
Council of Constance; and Savonarola (1452–1498), who strove to snatch
Florence from the tyranny of the Medici family and install the city of God,
was hanged and burned with two of his companions.[15]

As the sixteenth century opened, the venality of the pontifical court
and the debasement of the clergy were themes for satirists. Many Christians
began to consider Rome as Babylon and the Pope as the Antichrist. Until
this time, religious revolts, often complicated by national interests, led only
to local movements and peasant uprisings followed by brutal suppression
and suffering. There were non-schismatic priests and bishops within the
Church who sought reform, ashamed of the corruption of the papacy which
sacrificed spiritual authority for material interests. Other clergy, not tempt-
ed by internal reform, were attracted nonetheless to novel ideas which often

14. Pouzet, "Les origines lyonnaises de la secte des Vaudois," 5–6.

15. Stéphan, *L'Épopée huguenote*, 11–21.

condemned them to the same fate as heretics. The monk Jean de Caturce was burned to death at Toulouse in 1532, and a former inquisitor, Louis Rochette, was executed in 1538 for proclaiming his new-found faith.[16] In its wake, "the Reformation manifestly split the ecclesiastical structure of the Middle Ages and thereby shattered the framework of that society called Christendom."[17] The Reformation would sweep across Europe and bring about violence and transformation on an unprecedented scale.

Christianity in France was far from being united and strong at the dawn of the Reformation. Elton asserts that "Luther did not assail a well-ordered society but one in the throes of moral decay and spiritual doubt; and he was not alone in recognising these weaknesses."[18] The Church appeared too closely tied to the nobility, too distant from the issues confronting common people, and blind and deaf to the need for spiritual reformation and socio-economic reform. Skepticism and criticism grew toward the Church's authority and dogmatic assertions. Although superstition abounded in the diverse expressions of Catholicism, advances in adult literacy led to contempt for untrained priests, and "fiscal privileges enjoyed by the clergy were a source of particular irritation."[19] In urban areas of France in the 1520s and 1530s "a fundamental sense of restlessness may be detected within the newly-emerging literate *bourgeoisie*."[20] This instability and disenchantment of the times permitted Protestantism to progressively gain a foothold without meeting the resistance that a united and respected Catholicism would have provided.[21] The monarchy and Gallican wing of the French Church sought greater autonomy from Rome and were opposed by the Ultramontane faction. Historically, there were two forms of Gallicanism. The ecclesiastical form affirmed the autonomy of the French Church from Rome. The political form emphasized the authority of the French king over the temporal organization of the French Church.[22] Ultramontanism referred to a movement that supported the traditional position of the Italian Church concerning the absolute power of the Pope. This infighting heightened tensions and suspicions between Rome and France. The division and quests

16. Miquel, *Guerres de religion*, 154–55.

17. Bainton, *Reformation of the Sixteenth Century*, 4.

18. Elton, *Reformation Europe*, 125.

19. McGrath, *Life of Calvin*, 9.

20. McGrath, *Life of Calvin*, 176.

21. Bloch, *Réforme Protestante*, 7.

22. CNEF, *Laïcité française*, 12–13.

for power provided fertile soil in diverse intellectual and religious milieux, at least initially, for the new religious ideas which came from Germany.[23]

Luther's early writings were eagerly received in France before being condemned by the Sorbonne in 1521.[24] His writings spread so widely that they were soon censured and publicly burned. It was at this time that those who spoke about the Reformation, or were designated for persecution by the inquisitors, were called "Lutherans" regardless of their connection with Luther.[25] Beginning in 1523 those who embraced the new teachings were pursued and many put to death as heretics. The first "Lutheran" was burned alive at the stake in Paris in August 1523, an Augustinian monk named Jean Vallière. By the simple fact of their existence, Protestants challenged the authority of the king and the principle of ecclesiastical privilege in their attack against the first privileged order, the Church of France.[26] It became clear in France early on that the Catholic Church wanted no part in a Reformation which threatened both the privileged Church and the increasingly authoritarian State on the path to absolute monarchism.

By 1530, other Reformers, united by their common hatred for the papacy, albeit with doctrinal disagreements, had stirred controversy and brought upheaval throughout Europe. Ulrich Zwingli (1484–1531) drove the Swiss into religious wars and won over Zurich, Berne, and Bale to the Reformation. The theologian Johannes Oecolampadius (1482–1531) assisted Zwingli in convincing the citizens of Bale to break with Rome. The imperial city of Strasbourg was equally converted to the Protestant cause thanks to the efforts of Martin Bucer (1491–1551). French believers were attracted to Strasbourg which welcomed them when persecution began in the 1520s and later found refuge there when persecution intensified in the 1540s.[27] These challenges to Rome's religious hegemony led to increasing hostilities and repression and were foreboding precursors to the Wars of Religion. The tyrannical tendencies of the powerful French monarchy and complicit Church were unmistakably seen in their united response to *l'affaire des placards* in 1534 and 1535. Placards smuggled in from Switzerland were posted on walls around Paris to denounce the mass as sorcery. The leaders

23. Baubérot and Carbonnier-Burkard, *Histoire des Protestants*, 13.

24. Diefendorf, *Beneath the Cross*, 49.

25. Elton, *Reformation Europe*, 81.

26. Bost, *Histoire des Protestants*, 29.

27. Miquel, *Guerres de religion*, 28–29.

of the Sorbonne had already convinced François I (1494–1547)[28] that in Germany, where many princes had embraced the teachings of Luther, there was no longer a true Christian church, or government, or marriage, and that people lived as they pleased in a debauched, lawless manner. They persuaded the king that Protestants wanted to provoke an uprising in France with the placards. From this moment on, François I consented to brutal measures to suppress the heretics with widespread persecution. In response to the placards, an elaborate procession against the heretics was organized in January 1535 during which at least twenty heretics were burned to death and scores of others fled the city.[29] The procession advanced throughout the city with royal princes, numerous relics, and reliquary caskets including those of Saint Marcel and Saint Geneviève. The bishop of Paris carried "the Eucharist as [the procession's] central metaphor and eucharistic devotion its primary gesture," and was followed by the king walking alone "to present himself as a solitary and humble Christian."[30] L'affaire des placards "marked the termination of Lutheran success in France and, despite the later Calvinist explosion, the end of any hope that the Reformation might conquer that country."[31]

POLITICS AND RELIGIOUS WAR

The Wars of Religion cannot be divorced from political, socioeconomic, and military efforts to gain or retain power. Or in other words, the relationship gradually grew between religious aspirations and the political means to carry them out. Prior to the Wars of Religion there was little organized Protestant resistance to the State. The preaching of the gospel and the death of martyrs were persuasive in themselves and multitudes were won to the new faith. Many who embraced the teachings of Luther worked for reform within the Church. Others went further and embraced a new religion which placed them in opposition to the established political and ecclesiastical powers. One cannot always discern the motives for conversions to Protestantism. There were certainly genuine conversions and others tainted by self-interest. The politics of both Protestants and Catholics involved

---

28. French proper names will generally be used for French royalty instead of their English counterparts.

29. Bost, *Histoire des Protestants*, 44.

30. Diefendorf, *Beneath the Cross*, 46.

31. Elton, *Reformation Europe*, 80.

calling on foreign powers: Spain, Germany, Italy, and Switzerland for Catholics; mostly England and Lutheran princes in Germany for Protestants. The royal houses of France—Valois-Angoulême, Bourbon, Guise (branch of the house of Lorraine), Montmorency—were often in competition and made alliances according to political expediency. The house of Guise was the most ardent archenemy of Protestants, and its members became the architects of the Saint Bartholomew's Day massacre. The other royal families had members either converted to the Huguenot cause or were allied by marriage. Antoine de Bourbon married Jeanne d'Albret, queen of Navarre. Their son, the future Henri IV (1553–1610), married Marguerite de Valois, daughter of Catherine de Médicis and Henri II, and later married Marie de Médicis. Louis de Bourbon, prince of Condé (1530–1569), married Eléonore de Roye of the house of Montmorency. The marriages between royal families extended to England, Spain, Austria, and Italy, and other countries. François I, of the house of Valois, in his second marriage took as spouse Eléonore d'Autriche, sister of Charles V of Germany, and widow of Emmanuel, king of Portugal. François II married Mary Stuart, Queen of Scotland. Henri II married the Italian, Catherine de Médicis, niece of Pope Clement VII, and Charles IX married Elisabeth d'Autriche. The political intrigues, self-serving machinations, assassinations, and executions were never far from religious questions. François de Lorraine (1519–1563), also known as François de Guise, commander of French Catholic forces, was assassinated in 1563; Henri de Guise had Gaspard de Coligny assassinated in 1572; Henri de Guise and his brother Charles, the cardinal of Guise were assassinated by Henri III (1551–1589) in 1588, who himself was assassinated by a monk in 1589; Henri IV was assassinated in 1610 by a Catholic fanatic; kings Charles IX and Louis XIV had their subjects massacred, and they declared outlaws and traitors all those who did not embrace their Catholic faith. Louis XVI and his family were executed in 1793 by their subjects, and priests of the formerly triumphant Catholic confession fled into exile. In all this some saw the hand of God; others the hand of man.[32]

From a political perspective, as the Huguenot movement expanded and a Huguenot party emerged, the Huguenots were attacked as dangerous traitors and rebels for their alliances with foreign nations. Although they were charged with creating a State within the State, the accusation cuts both ways. In the sixteenth century the royal court was controlled for decades by an Italian, the cunning and ambitious Catherine de Médicis. We

32. Stéphan, *L'Épopée huguenote*, 146.

will also see that many of the Huguenot oppressors were foreign mercenaries—Germans, Swiss, Italians, Spanish—who burned, sacked, and pillaged their way through the provinces and villages, either as a reward or as salary for their services. When entreaties to the king failed to procure relief, the Huguenots were forced to defend hearth and home from invaders. When political solutions were unsuccessful and repression raged, the forced exile of Reformed pastors after the Revocation of the Edict of Nantes in 1685 led to the War of the Camisards. Self-proclaimed prophets arose claiming divine inspiration, and some of their followers committed inexcusable acts of revenge and slaughter. Protestant exiles, especially pastors, disapproved of these leaders and the bloodshed which often accompanied their reprisals. In spite of these excesses, the obstinate struggle of the Huguenot people, at times embellished with legend or misrepresented by their enemies, still provokes a wave of admiration throughout the world where their story is known. The Camisards remain great because their struggle was great.[33]

POLITICAL UNITY DISRUPTED

The Wars of Religion must also be understood in the context of times when warfare was ever present on the European continent as nation states competed for dominance, and the Holy Roman Empire fought with a vengeance against those who challenged her centuries-old authority and domination. The French king François I of the House of Valois-Angoulême was constantly at war with his principal and formidable adversary, Charles V (1500–1558), known also as Charles Quint, of the house of Hapsburg. Through his parents, Charles V inherited Spain, provinces in Holland, the kingdom of Naples, and possessions in Austria. In 1519 he was elected Holy Roman Emperor and became the most powerful monarch of the first half of the sixteenth century. He would be the last emperor to attempt the unity of Christendom under his empire as a counter to the growing threat of the Ottoman Empire in the Balkan and Mediterranean regions. His dream of unity would be frustrated by the French kings François I and Henri II (1519–1559) and challenged by the Protestant Reformation initiated by Luther.[34]

Charles V possessed the largest army in Europe at the time. France alone was able to stand against it with her well-organized artillery and

33. Stéphan, *L'Épopée huguenote*, 274.

34. Miquel, *Guerres de religion*, 26.

infantry which hailed primarily from the provinces of Picardy and Gascogne. François I went to war against the Swiss and took possession of Milan and Piedmont. His adversary Charles V could not allow these disruptions to go unanswered in regions sandwiched between his spheres of influence in Spain and Germany. For forty years war was waged between the houses of France and Austria (1519–1559). After the Battle of Pavia in 1525, François I lost Milan and was imprisoned at Madrid by Charles V. The children of François I were held as hostages and liberated only after a ransom payment. With the Peace of Madrid in 1526, France renounced her claim to Milan and Naples and the first phase of war between François I and Charles V ended.[35] Charles V won another victory in 1529 which ended with the Peace of Cambrai in 1529. Several years later when the French army invaded the states of the Duke of Savoy, Charles V responded by attacking Provence and Picardy. The pope proposed a truce between the belligerents but war broke out again in 1542, at which time the German states of Brandenburg and Saxony became Lutheran. A French victory in 1544 at Cérisoles forced Charles V to confirm the conditions of the Peace of Cambrai with the Peace of Crépy. He renounced his claims to Burgundy, although he was still strong enough to oblige François I to surrender claims to Naples, Flanders, and Artois.[36] The respite provided by the Peace of Crépy allowed Charles V to crush the German Protestant princes at the battle of Mühlberg in 1547. In this same year Henri II, the new king of France "set up a special court, the *chambre ardente*, to destroy the spread of Protestantism."[37] He annexed the three bishoprics (*Trois-Evêchés*) of Metz, Toul, and Verdun in 1552. Charles V was forced to abdicate in 1556 after failed attempts to recapture these cities, but not before signing the Peace of Augsburg in 1555 recognizing the plurality of religions in Germany and leaving Savoy and Piedmont to France. His son and successor to the Spanish empire, Philip II (1527–1598), avenged these defeats at the battle of Saint-Quentin in 1557 which forced Henri II to definitively renounce political intervention in Italy.[38]

The sound of fury during forty years of battle provides the background for the development of the Reformation in Europe. Charles V's dream of a universal monarchy was shattered and France secured her borders. The

35. Elton, *Reformation Europe*, 50.

36. Elton, *Reformation Europe*, 172.

37. Elton, *Reformation Europe*, 164.

38. Miquel, *Guerres de religion*, 27.

cost of wars weakened the French state, yet the construction of an absolute monarchy begun under Louis IX (1214–1270) continued unabated. Whatever internal and external struggles were endured, the French monarchy continued to reinforce its powers during the first half of the sixteenth century at the expense of clergy, nobles, privileged cities, and provincial states with crushing taxes. Royal vigilance and unity of the kingdom could not tolerate or accept, as in Germany, the secession of cities or provinces to religion. Repression of heresy became official policy and Protestant heretics had no right of legal existence. The seditious ideas of Luther, which entered the French kingdom in 1519 and had already disrupted Germany, would lead to waves of persecutions. The Reformation continued and expanded in France under John Calvin (1509–1564). Calvin's influence would soon eclipse that of Luther with the publication of his *Institutes*, in Latin in 1536 and in French in 1541. In a short time, the majority of French provinces were profoundly saturated by Calvinism. The first synod of the Reformed church took place in 1559, the same year as the Treaty of Cateau-Cambrésis which marked the end of the struggle between France and Spain for the control of Italy and "brought the age of Charles V to a close."[39] The royal power in France lost two battles at the same time: the battle against foreign adversaries and the battle against heresy. The kingdom was besieged from within by a foreign religion that could not be tolerated and thus must perish. A heavy price would be paid by those who dared resist.[40]

39. Elton, *Reformation Europe*, 193.
40. Miquel, *Guerres de religion*, 28–29.

Chapter 2

Disruptors of Religious Monopoly

THE SIXTEENTH-CENTURY REFORMERS WERE preceded by others who sought reform within the Catholic Church. As early as the twelfth century, Pierre Valdo (*Valdès*), known to us as Peter Waldo, took a vow of poverty confirmed by Pope Alexander III (p. 1159–1181), and became the leader of the Waldensians (*Vaudois*). They were truly forerunners of the Reformation who initially did not seek a rupture from the established Church or the establishment of a new sect.[1] They sought to purify and reform the Church from within with a return to apostolic teaching. Waldo and his followers were banned from preaching by Pope Lucius III (p. 1181–1185), banished, and then excommunicated at both the Council of Verona in 1184 and at the Council of Latran in 1215. Exiled from their city of Lyon, they spread to the valleys of Dauphiné and the Alpes of Piedmont, to Languedoc, and to Spain. The Inquisition did not spare them. Their children froze to death on mountain pastures and entire families were hunted and smoked out from mountain caves. Yet the Inquisition failed to stamp them out and the changing times provided new ways to communicate the teaching of others who sought reform and renewal both inside and outside the Church.[2]

The writings of heretics during medieval times were available only through the slow and faulty method of copying. The invention of the printing press by Gutenberg in 1450 allowed the mass distribution of new ideas in different languages. The printing press provided more security in the transmission of ideas and assured a rapid spread of the message which no

1. Pouzet, "Les origines lyonnaises de la secte des Vaudois," 33.
2. Leconte, *Sur les traces des vaudois*, 11–13.

medieval heretic could have ever imagined.[3] Its role in the propagation of Reformed teaching cannot be exaggerated. The dogmas and practices of the ancient Roman Church were challenged and questioned as never before. The Renaissance, begun in Italy in the last decade of the fourteenth century, had revolutionized the world of art and had been accompanied by humanism which revived interest in antiquity and ancient texts in Hebrew and Greek. Humanists like Lefèvre d'Étaples acquired knowledge of biblical languages, attempted to restore the foundation texts of Christianity to their original purity, and made them widely available to common people.[4] Martin Luther, Ulrich Zwingli, and John Calvin are undoubtedly the most well-known and most misunderstood Reformers. The influence of their pamphlets and books was such that in 1535 François I ordered the closure of all printshops in the kingdom.[5] There were other Reformers, including Theodore Beza (1519–1605), collaborator of Calvin; William (Guillaume) Farel (1489–1565) who fled to Switzerland in 1530 to escape persecution; and Philip Melanchthon (1497–1560), collaborator of Luther. They were all born and ministered at a time when the Catholic Church, which had amassed power and wealth, was spiritually bankrupt and would not attempt her own reformation until the Council of Trent in reaction to the work of the Reformers. Their lives, ministries, and influence have been debated, dissected, and even maligned. Whatever one's opinion of them, whatever motivated them, their sacrifices and impact were remarkable. The Reformers "thought of themselves as rebels but not as innovators, and in fact leveled the charge of innovation against the Church which had cast them out."[6] As Cameron asserts,

> The personal motives for the reformers' conversions are ultimately inexplicable. However, this overlooks the fundamental point: they were personal motives. One did not become a first-generation reformer by habit, compulsion, or default. Where any evidence exists, it suggests that the reformers reached their position only after serious and earnest heart-searching. They were some of the most conscientious revolutionaries ever to rebel against authority.[7]

3. Garrisson, *Histoire des protestants*, 23.

4. Garrisson, *Histoire des protestants*, 12.

5. Garrisson, *Histoire des protestants*, 42.

6. Bainton, *Reformation of the Sixteenth Century*, 5.

7. Cameron, *European Reformation*, 131.

MARTIN LUTHER

Martin Luther (1483–1546) was born in Saxony, Germany, the son of a miner. At the age of twenty-two he became a monk and entered the convent of Augustinians at Erfurt. One of Luther's contemporaries was Erasmus (1466-1536). They shared criticism of the Church and criticized each other. Erasmus criticized the scholasticism of his day and the contradiction between the teachings of Christ and the wealth and temporal power of the Church. His translation of the Greek New Testament in 1516 "did much to draw attention to the gulf between the contemporary and the original Church."[8] Yet he did not convert to the Protestant cause. Early on Luther accepted the Church's teaching that God gives grace to those who do their best. He gradually came to a clear understanding of the gospel and the doctrine of justification by grace through faith. According to Gerald Bray,

> It took a spiritual crisis in his own life to shake Luther out of this way of thinking. He did his best but discovered that it was not good enough. . . . After much searching, he found the answer in the words of the prophet Habakkuk, quoted by the apostle Paul in his letter to the Romans: 'the just shall live by faith' (Rom. 1:17; cf. Hab. 2:4). The scales dropped from his eyes as he realized that it is by grace that we are saved through faith and not by our works, however meritorious they are in themselves. The foundations of the old system were shaken to the root, and the result was the Protestant Reformation.[9]

Elton reminds us that "Luther did not just quarrel with the Church because he thought it diseased and corrupt: he thought it was unchristian and devilish."[10] Luther alleged that "the Church against which his critique was directed was only four hundred years old. The papal theocracy alone was the object of his attack, and his effort was to restore the Church of the Middle Ages."[11]

On October 31, 1517, Luther nailed his famous Ninety-Five Theses on the door of the Castle Church in Wittenberg and was ordered by the Church to recant his error or face excommunication, a fearful sentence which often carried with it the sentence of torture or death by civil magistrates. Rather

---

8. Elton, *Reformation Europe*, 13.

9. Bray, "Late-Medieval Theology," 93.

10. Elton, *Reformation Europe*, 196.

11. Bainton, *Reformation of the Sixteenth Century*, 5.

than recant, he burned the papal bull of excommunication which outlined his supposed errors. In 1520, he published writings against the tyranny of the pope. The popular support Luther enjoyed and his refusal to recant threatened the stability of the Holy Roman Empire. His early writings were read throughout France and other European nations. Among them were three Reformation treatises: *Letter to the Christian Nobility of the German Nation, On the Babylonian Captivity of the Church,* and *Freedom of a Christian.* The Sorbonne condemned his writings in Paris in 1521 and after this time the French who spoke of a Reformation were called "Lutherans." Summoned to the Diet of Worms called by Emperor Charles V, he was promised safe passage and held at the Episcopal Palace. Elton claims that "Luther's appearance at Worms proved to be the true beginning of the Reformation."[12] On the first day of his trial, April 17, 1521, John Eck asked him to renounce the errors in his published works. Luther requested a day for reflection and reappeared the next day to express his conviction of the ultimate authority of the Word of God to which he would submit. In defiance before German princes, bishops and lords, Luther proclaimed that he would only be persuaded by Holy Scriptures and would not violate his conscience, bound by the Scriptures.[13]

After several months hidden in the castle at Wartburg, Luther returned to Wittenberg to organize a new church in 1522 and German peasants embraced his message. The flames of this movement were fanned by prophetic extremism and the goal of some Anabaptists for renewal of the Church and State at the same time. Luther opposed these excesses which compromised the cause of the Reformation. Convinced that reforms could not be carried out apart from civil authorities, he took care that the new church was dependent on the State. He and his friends succeeded in organizing a church without pope, priests, or the mass. In 1525 the mass was abolished in Saxony, the veneration of saints and relics was suppressed, convents were opened, and marriage encouraged for the celibate. Germany at the time was divided into many small states and free cities which enabled the Reformation to spread in spite of Charles V's opposition. The Diet of Spire, with Catholics in the majority, was convoked in 1529 to stem the progress of Lutheranism. Those who affirmed that they would not consent to anything not found in the Holy Scriptures were called "Protestants" from this time onward. The teaching of Luther was summarized in the Confession of

12. Elton, *Reformation Europe,* 27.

13. Bost, *Histoire des Protestants,* 27–30.

Augsburg in 1530 by Luther's friend Melanchthon.[14] In short, "the papal, clerical theocracy was gone because the pope was not infallible and the clergy were not spiritually superior or more competent than laity."[15] Alister McGrath explains Luther's theological priority:

> For Luther, the reformation of morals and the renewal of spiri-
> tuality, although of importance in themselves, were of secondary
> significance in relation to the *reformation of Christian doctrine*
> (italics his). . . . For Luther, a reformation of morals was secondary
> to a reformation of doctrine.[16]

Among his many accomplishments, Luther translated the Greek New Testament into German in 1522 and the Hebrew Old Testament into German in 1534, the latter considered a foundational work for modern German. His translation work is considered his "supreme religious and literary achievement."[17] He is credited with establishing five fundamental principles or *solae: sola scriptura, sola fide, sola gratia, solus Christus*, and *soli Deo gloria*. These scriptural truths set his teaching apart from the teaching of the Church and announced an inevitable rupture.[18] He was also the reformer and founder of Christian singing in the Church. He opened the Bible as the only source from which hymns could spring. He wrote dozens of hymns with biblical and pious sentiments which nurtured the German soul.[19] Doumergue speaks of the slow birth of singing in Protestant churches as a chick emerging from its shell with the melody freed from clerical rigidity and monotony.[20] Luther's influence in France would soon be eclipsed by that of Calvin, but "without Luther there would still have been no Reformation."[21] At his death on February 18, 1546, "his gentle and assured departure consolidated the triumph of his life. He had never meant to break the Church or bring turmoil to the world, but the thrust within himself of what he conceived to be the truth had not let him rest."[22]

---

14. Bost, *Histoire des Protestants*, 31–32.

15. Bainton, *Reformation of the Sixteenth Century*, 52.

16. McGrath, *Luther's Theology*, 19–20.

17. Bainton, *Reformation of the Sixteenth Century*, 62.

18. Bloch, *Réforme Protestante*, 17–18.

19. Doumergue, *Le vrai chant*, 24.

20. Doumergue, *Le vrai chant*, 30.

21. Elton, *Reformation Europe*, 3.

22. Elton, *Reformation Europe*, 176.

ULRICH ZWINGLI

While Luther ministered in Germany, another Reformer, Ulrich Zwingli, spread Reformation teachings in Switzerland. He began his ministry as a priest at Glarus and eventually ministered at Zurich in 1519 where he started to preach through the New Testament. He preached as Luther did without knowing him personally and made the dubious assertion that "he had arrived at his theology independently of Luther."[23] Supported by the leaders of Zurich, Zwingli convoked priests to public discussions. In the years 1523 to 1525 he emerged victorious with the mass abolished in Zurich, church services conducted in the vernacular, new interpretations of baptism and the Lord's Supper proposed, statues removed, relics buried, and convents transformed into hospitals or schools. His reforms soon spread to Berne, Basel, and Strasbourg.[24]

Catholic cantons took up arms against Reformed cantons. Zwingli was killed in 1531 at the battle of Kappel, in which he took part as a chaplain for the troops from Zurich. Before his death Zwingli had hoped that regions and cities won to the Reformation would unite. But Luther had guarded a conception of the Lord's Supper which to Zwingli appeared too close to Catholic teaching. Both Reformers rejected transubstantiation as unscriptural. Yet Luther held to a real presence of Christ in the elements. Zwingli understood the Lord's Supper more symbolically and Luther ridiculed his interpretation.[25] This and other differences led to the independent development of the Reformation in Germany and Switzerland. The eastern frontiers of France, however, were now flanked by cities and countries where the Reformation had triumphed and from where teaching and books penetrated more deeply in France.[26] Although Zwinglianism faded in influence, "not only had Zwingli's Zürich been a forerunner of Calvin's Geneva, but the more gently human and humanistic traditions of Zwingli's teaching also modified the fundamental rigor of that Church's Calvinist basis."[27] The soil was prepared for the next great Reformer, John Calvin.

---

23. Elton, *Reformation Europe*, 39.

24. Elton, *Reformation Europe*, 40.

25. Elton, *Reformation Europe*, 43–45.

26. Bost, *Histoire des Protestants*, 32–33.

27. Elton, *Reformation Europe*, 46.

JOHN CALVIN[28]

Calvin was born in 1509 in Noyon, France in the region of Picardy. He received a classical education through which he acquired an encyclopedic knowledge of authors from antiquity and from the patristic period. He later studied law until the death of his father in 1531.[29] Elton asserts that "there are some indications that in 1533 Calvin underwent conversion in some form."[30] In 1536 he wrote the first edition in Latin of his *Institutes of the Christian Religion*, "which evolved through subsequent revisions into the most forceful and successful exposition of Reformed Protestantism of the sixteenth century."[31] The preface of the *Institutes*, dated in Basel by Calvin on August 1, 1535, was dedicated to the French king. Calvin courageously defended the martyrs associated with *l'affaire des placards* and demonstrated that Calvin had a plan to reform the Church.[32] The moment was well chosen. François 1 had recently released an edict of amnesty temporarily ending persecution and claimed there were no longer any heretics in France.[33] Several months later Calvin passed through Geneva where Farel had already abolished the mass but needed help to organize a new church. Both were briefly chased from Geneva in 1538 due to the religious laws Farel had imposed on the city. Calvin went to Strasbourg where he met the Reformer Martin Bucer (1491–1551). The French Reformation found early support at Strasbourg which was later reinforced at Geneva. The city was a refuge for the first reformed French Protestants and Calvin organized French refugees into the first French Reformed church. French Reformed churches modeled the Reformed community established at Strasbourg until the years 1550–1560.[34] It was at Strasbourg that he began writing his *Commentaries on the Bible*. Calvin returned to Geneva in 1541 where he ministered for twenty-three more years until his death in 1564. He also published his revised *Institutes* translated into French in 1541, soon condemned by the Paris parliament. The *Institutes* were "a landmark in the

---

28. See Alister McGrath's *A Life of John Calvin* for a detailed study of the person and ministry of Calvin.

29. Bloch, *Réforme Protestante*, 14.

30. Elton, *Reformation Europe*, 148–49.

31. Benedict and Reinburg, "Religion and the Sacred," 138.

32. Calvin, *L'Institution chrétienne*, XXXVIII.

33. Miquel, *Guerres de religion*, 108.

34. Garrisson, *Histoire des protestants*, 41.

history of French prose as well as French Protestantism."[35] Doctrines that became known as Calvinism were spread throughout Europe and beyond. Calvin called upon believers living in places with no Protestant church to separate from the Catholic Church and if necessary relocate to a place where they could worship freely.[36]

Calvin held the conviction that the Psalms of David were the most appropriate for singing in churches. When he arrived in Strasbourg he had in his possession twelve Psalms and subsequently translated others which led to the publication of a Psaltery in 1538.[37] Theodore Beza, friend and successor to Calvin, completed the work that Clémont Marot began years earlier, and in 1562 published the first editions of a complete Psalter with one hundred and fifty psalms.[38] As the Protestant church passed through centuries of persecution, of combat, of defeats, and of victories, these Psalms were unequalled in nurturing the soul of Huguenot people in their suffering. In their distress, after crushing defeats, abandoned by their friends and family, without hope of earthly deliverance, and at the moment of martyrdom, they sang these Psalms.[39] Reformed believers were not the only religious confession to resort to the Psalms throughout the centuries. What characterized the Huguenot psalter was the active and militant role it played in the diffusion of the Reformation and the edification of believers in the framework of a largely hostile kingdom.[40]

France obviously had a special place in Calvin's ministry and his influence there was immense. There are varying estimates of the number of Huguenot churches in France around 1562. There were 2,150 according to Admiral de Coligny, but more likely around 1,250 with over two million adherents out of a population numbering twenty million.[41] Calvin insisted each time he sent new pastors to France that they prohibit the faithful from engaging in acts of violence or challenging the authorities. He strove to calm the outbursts of passion and exhorted believers to be content with private worship as long as public worship was not permitted. He condemned the anarchist attitude of former monks who had embraced his

---

35. Elton, *Reformation Europe*, 163.

36. Bost, *Histoire des Protestants*, 45.

37. Doumergue, *Le vrai chant*, 39–40.

38. Doumergue, *Le vrai chant*, 45.

39. Doumergue, *Le vrai chant*, 41.

40. Zuber, "Les psaumes," 350.

41. McGrath, *John Calvin*, 191–92.

teachings, and whose sermons questioned the social and political order. It was decided that former monks seeking pastoral designation needed to first receive the authorization of a synod rather than the approval of a few ministers. Regional synods also had the authority to depose pastors for heresy who no longer enjoyed the confidence of Geneva. In his writings, Calvin made it clear that resistance to the gospel should be expected, that believers should not be cowardly or fearful, and that God would laugh at the inevitable calamity of their enemies.[42] Calvin roundly criticized those guilty of insurrection against the king and the kingdom, whether fanatics acting in the name of the gospel or because of their opposition to the superstitions of Rome. He expressed his wish that believers devote themselves to the king and to the God who seated him on the royal throne.[43] Yet within fifteen years after Calvin's death, "in the hands of French Huguenots and English puritans, Calvinism became a source of anti-authoritarian and libertarian thinking."[44]

Calvin was aware of persecution taking place in France as seen in many of his letters. In June 1552 Calvin wrote to five young French men held as prisoners in Lyon; Martial Alba of Montauban, Pierre Escrivain of Gascogne, Charles Faure of Blauzac in Angoumois, Pierre Navihères of Limousin, and Bernard Seguin of Réole. They had been students at Lausanne, dedicated to the ministry, and willing to return to their country to serve God and churches. On their way to France they spent two days in Geneva before continuing on to Lyon. They accepted an invitation to visit the home of someone they met along the way, were arrested and imprisoned. The church of Geneva worked tirelessly for their release and testified of their concern through the letters of Calvin. His first letter assured them of the prayers of God's people, that they were not forgotten, and messages had been sent to French authorities to obtain their release. He also addressed doctrinal questions, closed with a prayer for their protection and for the fullness of the Spirit, and that the name of Christ be glorified through them for the edification of his church.[45] Another letter was written in September 1553 after the students were declared guilty of heresy, were delivered to the secular authorities for judgment, and made an appeal to the Parliament of Paris. They had been moved from dungeon to dungeon, returned to Lyon

42. Miquel, *Guerres de religion*, 185–86.
43. Calvin, *Lettres*, 265–67.
44. Elton, *Reformation Europe*, 167.
45. Calvin, *Lettres*, 340–45.

from Paris, and awaited their sentence. On March 1, 1553, they received the ruling that they would die at the stake. The news spread to Lausanne and Geneva and caused great sorrow. Calvin encouraged them in the midst of what might be their last combat that the grace of God and the Spirit would sustain them to the end.[46] Just before their death, Calvin wrote another letter in May 1553. Still hopeful for their release, he recognized that God might have chosen to use their death as a testament to the truth. When the condemned came to the place of execution, they mounted the pile of wood with cheerful hearts. The last one to take his place was Martial Alba, the oldest of the five, who had been kneeling in prayer. He made a request to the Lieutenant Tignac to kiss his brothers before he died. His request was granted and as he kissed each one he said, *Adieu, adieu, mon frère*. The fire was lit and the voices of the five martyrs were heard encouraging one another with the words: *Courage, mes frères, courage*. They were the last words of the Lord's martyrs.[47] After their deaths, Calvin wrote other prisoners in July 1563 at Lyon to console them. Among them were Denis Peloquin of Blois and Louis de Marsac of Bourbonnais. Marsac responded to Calvin thanking him for letters sent to Peloquin which were shared with other prisoners, and asked him to persevere in prayer for them. Calvin expressed both his sadness at the news of their arrest and his resignation to the sovereignty of God who would be glorified in their death.[48] Calvin himself "endured the trials of his ministry with unswerving determination and even refused to take obvious opportunities for ending his work at Geneva."[49] He died in 1564 shortly after the beginning of the Wars of Religion.

The arrival of the Reformation in Europe with its emphasis on the authority of Scripture, the priesthood of the believer and the freedom of conscience, and Renaissance humanism with its emphasis on individual autonomy, undermined the Church's grip on European society. Whereas Christian humanism in its noble goal of reform from within the Church "never made the slightest impact on the great mass of Christians of all degrees," Luther "started from a different and more revolutionary position."[50] According to Elton, the "restoration of God at the heart of religion and

---

46. Calvin, *Lettres*, 371–74.

47. Calvin, *Lettres*, 382–86.

48. Calvin, *Lettres*, 395–98.

49. Elton, *Reformation Europe*, 156.

50. Elton, *Reformation Europe*, 201.

theology was the positive theological achievement of the Reformation."[51] The Reformation developed with differences in different nations. "In many instances a new variety of the Reform arose independently for the simple reason that reform was so drastically needed."[52] Eugène Réveillard, deputy of Charente-Inférieure, wrote in 1907 that the Reformation, in the measure it brought back religion and Christian churches to the purity of their origins according to the intention of the Reformers, marked the beginning of the restoration of the principles of freedom of conscience and of worship, and at the same time, the separation of powers—civil and ecclesiastical.[53]

The restoration of these principles in France would not find ready acceptance among political and religious authorities. The privileged Catholic Church of the sixteenth century refused reformation and instead instituted systematic persecution and repression to silence the heretics, who in fact were faithful witnesses to the truth of God's Word. There would be decades of bloodshed in France as the lords of Church and State combatted religious liberty and freedom of conscience. Too much was at stake, too much to lose, to allow the subjects of these two entities a breath of freedom from relentless oppression and cruelty. Kings and bishops in an unholy alliance would resist all attempts to throw off their yokes of bondage. Fields and cities would run red with blood in attempts to extirpate Protestant heretics who refused to recant or allow their consciences to be enslaved. Some may question the extreme measures and violence that accompanied the Reformation but "it is fair to say that toleration, diversity of opinion, and respect for free consciences could not develop until the monolithic power of the Church had been broken."[54]

Five hundred years later, the Reformation's historical and religious importance cannot be exaggerated even if, as some claim, "from the very beginning of the writing of its history, the Reformation has been subject to the hopes, dreams, and distortions of its historians."[55] It is far beyond the scope of this book to enter into the subjects of changing perspectives, competing narratives, denials of providence and divine intervention, and confessional polemics about the Reformation. What is unarguable is that "no other movement of religious protest or reform since antiquity has been

51. Elton, *Reformation Europe*, 197.

52. Bainton, *Reformation of the Sixteenth Century*, 77.

53. Réveillard, *La séparation*, 23.

54. Elton, *Reformation Europe*, 200.

55. Dixon, "Martin Luther and the Reformation," 404–5.

so widespread or lasting in its effects, so deep and searching in its criticism of received wisdom, so destructive in what it abolished or so fertile in what it created."[56] Cameron contends that although there were reformations throughout Europe in Catholic nations, Reformation in the singular is reserved "for a particular process of change, integrating cultural, political, and theological factors in a way never seen before and rarely since."[57] Walker recognizes that the "defensive action to the Protestant threat is appropriately called the Counter-Reformation" and also that "one may properly speak of an indigenous Catholic Reformation of the sixteenth century."[58] Yet the localized attempts at "spiritual renewal would not have won the support of popes and prelates—would not have been 'institutionalized,' so to speak—were it not for the profound shock administered to the church at large by the Protestant Reformation."[59] The Catholic Church may have experienced reforms, renewals or reformations in areas of practice, piety, and missionary zeal, but did not experience Reformation in the weighty sense of the word which describes the reestablishment of apostolic doctrine. The Reformers proclaimed the divine authority of the Scriptures and encouraged personal Bible reading. Consequently, there was no longer one authoritative voice and interpreter of the Holy Scriptures. As people began reading the Christian Scriptures for themselves the divide between ecclesiastical authority and the faithful grew. Violence between rival confessions, complicated by political aspirations, became inevitable and led to repression and persecution. One of the major themes linking the various expressions of the Reformation was "the explosive and renovating and often disintegrating effect of the bible [sic], put into the hands of the commonalty and interpreted no longer by the well-conditioned learner, but by the faith and delusion, the common sense and uncommon nonsense, of all sorts of men."[60]

In light of the suffering and bloodshed associated with the Reformation, questions have been raised about the Reformation's necessity or inevitability. Many causes surely contributed to the Reformation—fear of death heightened by plagues, clergy abuses, economic uncertainty, and Renaissance influences. In addition, the weight of the Church's functions

56. Cameron, *European Reformation*, 1.

57. Cameron, *European Reformation*, 1.

58. Walker et al., *History of the Christian Church*, 502.

59. Walker et al., *History of the Christian Church*, 502.

60. Elton, *Reformation Europe*, 28–29.

in education and medical care for the population strained the Church's re-sources. In short, with the tasks assumed by this monopoly for hundreds of years, the Church became an institution in difficulty, outdated by cultural and social evolution, and no longer adapted to the times.[61] But in the end, "such questions cannot be answered with any degree of confidence. The fact remains, however, that Luther himself regarded the Reformation as having begun over, and to have chiefly concerned, the correct understanding of the Christian doctrine of justification."[62] The Reformation restored the Bible to a central place in culture and religion, and Reformed believers suffered and fought for the principle of freedom of conscience and of worship.

61. Garrisson, *Histoire des protestants*, 22.

62. McGrath, *Luther's Theology*, 21–22.

Chapter 3

Sixteenth-Century Repression and Persecution

As the Reformation developed in France, there were several periods in the first half of the sixteenth century of repression and persecution followed by amnesties, calls for abjuration, and a return to the Catholic faith. These were not wars in the strict sense of the word but times of great hardship, deprivation, confiscation, atrocities, and persecution against those who embraced new Protestant religious teachings. Many regions of France were affected by the arrival of new teachings, and people began to question the authority of the Church. Even worse in the eyes of the Church, those burdened by taxes both in times of plenty and famine refused to pay the tithe (*la dîme*) to absentee bishops. The repressions were often an excuse to dispossess peasants of their property and enrich nobles and clergy alike. Peasant resistance was often courageous yet in vain against trained soldiers and ruthless mercenaries. There were unspeakable atrocities, and it is true that Reformed believers in their desire for revenge were at times guilty of violence. Yet any unbiased reading of history reveals that there is no equivalency between the crimes of the Church and monarchy, and the acts of retaliation of those persecuted. This observation is true both on the scale of the violence and the depth of depravity in the unspeakable horrors inflicted on people who wanted only to follow the teachings of a religion perceived as hostile to the monarchy and as competition to the powerful, established Church.

REFORMATION AWAKENING AT MEAUX

Much of the early violence took place at Meaux where preachers provoked the ire of the Sorbonne and drew growing hostility from parliamentarians. The preachers were guilty of subversive actions of advancing literacy in order that common people might read the Gospels and recite the Creed in French. William Farel and the Leclerc brothers contested the veneration of Mary and the saints. Farel was considered dangerous because of his teaching opposing purgatory. Their followers were soon called Lutherans even if they had little contact with the German Reformation; Lutherans were anyone suspected of heresy.[1]

To understand this turn of events we must begin with Guillaume Briçonnet II, named bishop at the age of seventeen. He had followed in the steps of his father, Cardinal Briçonnet, who left Rome in 1510 with four other cardinals to launch reforms in the Church in opposition to Pope Julius II (1443–1513). Guillaume entered Meaux in 1516 as the new bishop with full knowledge of the subterfuges and quarrels of the Church. He was a confidant of François I whose impressive victory "over the combined papal and Swiss forces at Marignano in September 1515 established him as a force to be reckoned with in Italian affairs, and enhanced his authority over the French church."[2] The religious positions of François seemed to fluctuate between his intolerant counselors and his sister Marguerite who later became an adherent of Reformed teaching. Yet he was most preoccupied with his royal authority, favorable to the spirit of the Renaissance but opposed to the moral rigorism of Lefèvre and Briçonnet. Professors and legal experts proclaimed that the king was the vicar of Christ, the oldest son of the Church, and king by the grace of God. Several months after his enthronement in 1515, François I sent Briçonnet to Rome to negotiate the Concordat of Bologna with Pope Leo X (1475–1521). The Concordat removed from the French Church its traditional rights of election and accorded the king the right of appointment to major ecclesiastical positions, placing the high clergy and nobility under his control. He was able to reward his most faithful servants in offering them abbeys, bishoprics, titles, and other benefits. If this Concordat encountered opposition, if it pushed some clergy toward the Reformation because of scandalous nominations, it yet accomplished François I's aim to attach French royalty to the Catholic Church with the

---

1. Miquel, *Guerres de religion*, 10.
2. McGrath, *John Calvin*, 12.

guarantee of a Catholic monarchy. German princes favorably welcomed the ideas of Luther and saw a rupture with the Church the occasion to throw off her yoke and to seize the clergy's possessions. François saw his best interests fulfilled in conserving a regime which strengthened his power.[3]

At this epoch, the Church was the largest landholder in France. The king with his new concordataire authority sought to establish an inventory and exercise more control of the Church's possessions acquired over the fifty previous years. The king and bishops along with municipal leaders shared the jurisdiction of many cities, including Meaux, and benefited from the revenue obtained through taxes and fines. The king did not contest the seigneurial rights of the bishops. Although he sought to eventually recuperate land for himself, he was also interested in participating in the revenue received by the clergy. The traffic of indulgences was a considerable source of revenue. An indulgence was a remission of the sentence granted sinners in exchange for payment. The remission could be total or partial depending on the amount paid. The anguish was so intense at the beginning of the sixteenth century that this traffic organized by the pope paid handsomely. The money placed in trunks permitted souls to fly from purgatory to paradise. The clergy was known for its corruption and loose morals, and high dignitaries of the Church often had large families. This took place without seeming scandalous.[4]

Briçonnet inherited a bishopric not unlike many others in France, where people panicked at the thought of dying without the last rites, where apart from the threatenings of hell and damnation there was little Bible knowledge, where the Virgin was solicited for all their needs, and each saint had its specialty. Sacred relics imported from the Holy Land after the crusades were treated as talismans and God was mostly forgotten in the pantheon of saints. The naïve faith of the people and their credulity was largely the fault of a deficient clergy which either could not or would not provide serious religious instruction. Briçonnet had taken note of these deficiencies in his diocese and set out to correct them. Imagine the surprise when the newly-installed bishop began to investigate the morality of the priests who he considered lost children of a sick Church. He gathered a group of priests in 1518, spoke to them clearly about the dire situation, and became indignant at their indifference. New preachers were hired as evangelists and sent to parishes to awaken consciences to new life. A year

3. Stéphan, *L'Épopée huguenote*, 34–36.

4. Miquel, *Guerres de religion*, 33–39.

later, with discouraging results, Briçonnet decided to train new priests and pursue his project of reform. He knew that a reform of customs and mores was useless apart from a reform of the inner man. To that end, he turned to Lefèvre d'Étaples of Picardy.[5]

LEFÈVRE D'ÉTAPLES

Since 1505 Lefèvre had been in contact with Briçonnet. It seemed natural for Briçonnet to call him to Meaux which became the principal place of activity for the *"évangéliques."*[6] Lefèvre organized a group of friends to attempt the reform of a Church which continued to accumulate privileges and distanced herself from the great multitudes of the faithful. Lefèvre was a contemporary of Erasmus and had a passion to bring the Scriptures to everyone in their own language. For some, he appeared factious and dangerous and was surveilled for his attachment to the truths of the Bible. He raised the question on which all the Reformers would take a position some-day—the relationship between faith and works in justification.[7] His exhortation for all Christians to read and meditate on the Gospels was opposed to the Church's position that the intelligence of laics could never sound the sublime depths of Scripture. On this essential point the Catholic Church and different streams of Reformation thought radically diverged. For the Church, the truth resided in indisputable dogmas established by tradition. For the Reformers, the authority resided in Scripture and every believer had the right and the duty to search and understand its truths. Adversaries at the Sorbonne, or more precisely at the Faculté de théologie de Paris, treated Lefèvre with contempt. But the opposition did not stop Parisian students from visiting Meaux, attracted by the teaching of Lefèvre.[8]

There were other notable visitors at Meaux such as Marguerite d'Alençon and her queen mother, Louise de Savoie, wife of Charles de Valois (1459–1496). Marguerite, sister of François I, became queen of Navarre in 1527 and figured as the guardian angel of the evangelicals. From all appearances she discovered the teaching of justification by faith and experienced a genuine religious conversion. Her writings and her poetry testify of her spiritual sensitivity accompanied by her charitable works. Her poetic work

5. Miquel, *Guerres de religion*, 40–46.

6. Stéphan, *L'Épopée huguenote*, 26.

7. Garrisson, *Histoire des protestants*, 33.

8. Stéphan, *L'Épopée huguenote*, 36–37.

shows the influence of Calvin, as in her poem, *Le triomphe de l'agneau* (The triumph of the Lamb) where she alludes to the elect: *Or, il a donc prédestiné les siens,* (Now, he has predestined his own); *Pour leur donner à jouir de ses biens.* (To give them the enjoyment of His possessions). She ardently desired the reform of the Church. Even when attacked by the Sorbonne, she guarded the hope of a reform wrought at the interior of the Church.[9]

The ideas of Lefèvre grew in the bishopric as he argued passionately for a return to apostolic teaching and denounced the veneration of saints and the sale of indulgences. Under royal protection by Marguerite, Lefèvre and his friends engaged in their missionary work. His *Commentarii initiatorii in quatuor Evangelia* appeared in 1522. Lefèvre translated the New Testament (1523) and Old Testament (1525) into French.[10] Marguerite wrote to Briçonnet that her brother the king and her mother were eager to know God's truth and to reform the Church. Lefèvre wrote Farel that François I himself had removed obstacles to reading the New Testament, now translated in French, every Sunday and holidays. In spite of impediments from the Sorbonne, the writings of Lefèvre were widely diffused in Picardy. At this stage, Luther was hardly known in France even if the events of 1517 at Wittenberg and Luther's excommunication had been communicated by travelers.[11]

Lefèvre, of course, was aware of the reforms carried out by Luther in Germany and Zwingli in Switzerland. By 1521 the group at Meaux had procured and were discussing some of Luther's writings. Lutheran teachings were condemned by the Sorbonne that same year which opened the way for an era of violence.[12] Lefèvre was not a schismatic and sincerely wished to revive a spirit of true worship within the Church. With conviction he sought to combat the traditions surrounding Saint Anne and Mary Magdalene. Yet, he revered the Virgin and the saints and began to exercise a great influence over many of his contemporaries including Bishop Briçonnet. Briçonnet, faithful servant of the king, understood that he needed to distance himself from those associated with Germany. At the same time,

9. Stéphan, *L'Épopée huguenote*, 27–31.

10. Stéphan, *L'Épopée huguenote*, 25–26. Garrisson dates the translation of the New Testament and Old Testament to 1524 and 1530 respectively (*Histoire des protestants*, 33).

11. Miquel, *Guerres de religion*, 51–52.

12. Miquel, *Guerres de religion*, 53.

he sought to reform his diocese in according importance to preaching the gospel.[13]

The condemnation of Luther by the pope was a fact that Bishop Briçonnet could not ignore. Friends of Lefèvre began to defect and returned to the teaching of the Church. Briçonnet did not wish to end his efforts of reform and decided to publicly condemn Luther in order to avoid his own condemnation. To placate the Sorbonne, edicts were announced in October 1523 which forbade the purchase or reading of Luther's writings. These repressive measures did not deter the people of Meaux who showed even more interest in the new teachings. All the while, Briçonnet continued to print and distribute the Gospels in French. His adversaries began a violent campaign against the bishop. Posters were hung from the cathedral in 1524 attacking Briçonnet as a Lutheran. In December of that same year, Briçonnet was called upon to post papal bulls of Pope Clement VII (1478–1534) which included the announcement of new indulgences. As a result, the people of Meaux were indignant, Farel was exiled, the posters ripped down, and the pope reviled as Antichrist. The city of Meaux entered into rebellion against the Church. In the absence of François I, prisoner of Charles V after the defeat at the Battle of Pavia, the first persecution was unleashed. At Meaux, Briçonnet acted in vain to calm the spirits. He instructed the priests to read prayers once again for the dead and to invoke the Virgin and saints, and took under his own protection the statues and images of saints. With the warnings of the bishop no longer respected by the people, the time of martyrs arrived, and the time of revolt.[14]

Persecution struck throughout France in the king's absence as his mother, Louise de Savoie, yielded to pressure from the Sorbonne and the Parliament. Jean Leclerc, arrested at Metz for destroying statues, had his right hand cut off, and his nose and nipples torn off with pincers. As he was carried to the fire, he sang Psalm 115:4, "Their idols are silver and gold, the work of human hands."[15] The search for more heretics began, and the group at Meaux was warned that they no longer enjoyed official protection. Arrests followed and Lefèvre fled in exile. At Meaux the combat for the gospel continued and the stories of martyrs served as fodder for sermons. In 1528 a large crowd gathered at the cathedral and posted a bull in French to the glory of Luther, allegedly signed by the pope. Briçonnet was scandalized

---

13. Stéphan, *L'Épopée huguenote*, 26–27.

14. Miquel, *Guerres de religion*, 54–58.

15. Doumergue, *Le vrai chant*, 42.

and searched for the authors of this outrage. Eight persons were delivered to him. Six were condemned, branded with the fleur de lys on the forehead, and led through the streets for three days. One recalcitrant cried aloud that the mass was a renouncement of the death and passion of Christ. He was dragged through the streets on a rack before being burned alive. Voilà, Briçonnet at the side of executioners.[16]

Briçonnet himself did not escape censure by Parliament for having permitted heresy to propagate at Meaux. Other bishops severely judged the events at Meaux and laid the blame on him. Although Briçonnet had not protected the extremists who had sought to abolish the hierarchy, had questioned the sacraments, and had destroyed statues, he was accused of having permitted the so-called Lutherans to organize and freely express their views. The attack on the hierarchy was unforgivable in the eyes of those who risked losing their privileges and temporal power. The bishops who gathered in 1528 at the Council of Sens demanded condemnation and punishment of the heretics at Meaux. The absolute value of all the sacraments, the adoration of Mary and veneration of the saints, and the necessity of good works for salvation were reaffirmed. The bishops reminded the king that his predecessors had not hesitated to use the sword to exterminate heresies. This call to repression was soon answered on May 31, 1528. An anonymous, iconoclastic Parisian cut off the head of a statue of Mary with the baby Jesus in her arms. The king placed a bounty on the head of the perpetrator. The guilty one not being found, an eminent person was arrested and burned at the stake, the humanist Louis Berquin. It was the first execution of a person of renown. Briçonnet died in 1534 without witnessing the martyrdom of the last members of the circle of Meaux, by all accounts numbering in the hundreds. Neither the censure nor the stake could prevent the evangelists of Meaux from inserting themselves in the rebellion and the Reformation. Lefèvre and Briçonnet had not been able to preserve the illusion that one could evangelize without calling into question the order of the kingdom. At this time in France, there did not exist Protestant principalities as in Germany, and Reformed believers had little protection. They needed to emigrate or hide. Lefèvre, for his part, found refuge with Marguerite d'Angoulême, now queen of Navarre. He died in his sleep, afflicted that he had not merited the fate of those slain for the confession of the gospel that he taught them.[17]

16. Miquel, *Guerres de religion*, 58–59.

17. Miquel, *Guerres de religion*, 60–63.

WALDENSIANS (VAUDOIS)

Of the many regions afflicted by persecution, the Luberon region in southern France was an early example, one that would be multiplied in the years to come. The Vaudois were considered by some the spiritual descendants of the twelfth-century Pierre Valdo. They lived in peace in the sheltered valleys of the Luberon where they had drained the swamps and cultivated lands belonging to Italian lords. It is said that people inhabiting the plains feared the Vaudois who had a reputation as sorcerers and married among themselves. At that time, they had spiritual leaders (*barbes*) who had authority over the people. The *barbes* were considered wise and venerable, and mysterious power was attributed to them. Their brothers in Dauphiné had previously suffered persecution and many had fled to Luberon for safety. The archbishop of Aix worried that this concentration of heretics might embrace the Reformation. Around 1530, Jean de Roma, who had already ravaged Meaux, was sent to investigate the Vaudois, committed atrocities against them, and enriched himself at their expense. As a result of this initial violence, two Vaudois, known as Maurel and Masson, crossed the frontiers to Alsace and Switzerland to confer with Reformed leaders. They were persuaded of the need to reform their beliefs, to definitively break with papist superstitions, and were sent back with two letters for their brothers in Mérindol. Only Maurel arrived home safely; Masson was arrested and burned alive at Dijon. A decisive meeting took place in Piedmont in 1532 with Vaudois leadership from different regions in which Farel convinced them to preserve only two sacraments without the mystical sense given by the Catholic Church: baptism and the Eucharist. Farel welcomed them to the Reformed faith with enthusiasm and called them the "elder sons of the Reformation."[18]

MÉRINDOL MASSACRE

With their integration into a larger European movement, the Vaudois no longer felt isolated. They welcomed all who sought refuge in their mountains, in particular apostate priests, valued for their literacy. The papal enclave Venaissin bordered this region. The pope, out of fear that the new religion would propagate, offered a plenary indulgence to all the Vaudois who abjured within two months. At the same time, his soldiers seized

18. Miquel, *Guerres de religion*, 119–21.

women and children to convert them forcibly. In 1532, young women were abducted in the village of Cabrières-du-Comtat. Their fathers, armed with clubs and pitchforks, were no match for the soldiers and were stopped without difficulty. The news circulated throughout the village and a mob emerged leading to the death of an official in Agoult and a judge in Apt. Pope Clement VII wrote the king of France to report the violence taking place at the door of papal states. François I gave instructions to the Parliament at Aix to intervene resulting in seven Vaudois burned at the stake, including one *barbe*. The intrusion of the king had the effect of pushing communities to revolt and many no longer paid their tithe to the clergy. The bishops of Sisteron, Apt, and Cavaillon feared this movement spreading throughout Provence and the most active Vaudois were imprisoned, some executed. It is estimated that about six thousand men belonged to the Vaudois sect at this time. Many were pursued and arrested because they denied purgatory, did not pray to saints, and refused to pay the tithe. The Vaudois, infuriated by the actions of ecclesiastical tribunals, took up arms, and assaulted prisons in Apt, Cavaillon, and Roussillon to liberate their brothers. The king, informed of these events, offered clemency to the heretics and the release of all not-yet-liberated prisoners on the condition that they abjure within six months. Not one person accepted his proposition and in 1538 the king ordered the arrest of the heretics and the confiscation of their possessions. Rumors reached the Parliament that the Vaudois were preparing for a siege and had stored stocks of powder and arms. Over one hundred fifty Vaudois were arrested, fourteen of them from Mérindol. A judge in Apt proceeded to arrest a miller and confiscated the mill after his execution. The inhabitants of Mérindol retaliated in taking up arms, burned the mill to the ground, pillaged farms, and stole sheep along the way. Nineteen residents of Mérindol were designated for arrest, some with their entire family based on absurd denunciations. As a climate of panic reigned in Aix, more unsubstantiated rumors circulated that the Vaudois were building forts in the forests, and that there were six hundred men in Mérindol armed with arquebuses, a type of long gun. The exaggerated total number swelled to eight thousand combatants. Soon after the arrest order was given, which included the seizure of pregnant women. But before it was carried out, the parliamentarians realized they had been played. In reality the Mérindoliens had fled to their mountains to avoid arrest after learning that on November 18, 1540, an order had been given condemning nineteen of them to be burned at the stake in three different places—Tourves,

Apt, and Aix—, that all their houses in Mérindol would be demolished, the place rendered uninhabitable, the woods around them destroyed, and their possessions confiscated. For the first time in the history of the Wars of Religion, the extirpation of heresy and the elimination of all heretics was undertaken.[19]

Farel, warned by courier of the order, immediately contacted Swiss and German cities in order to intercede diplomatically with the king. François I took this action into account and charged the governor of Piedmont, Guillame du Ballay, to investigate the Vaudois. When he delivered a favorable report, the king suspended the order and demanded the abjuration of the Vaudois elders within three months before the Parliament. Persecution was taking place throughout the kingdom and the king could not afford to handle the Vaudois lightly. On April 6, 1541, instead of sending the elders before the Parliament to abjure, the Mérindoliens sent their *barbes* to explain their faith in Jesus Christ and in the Scriptures, and to affirm their spirit of obedience to civil authorities. They submitted to all laws but requested that they be allowed to practice their faith without being constrained to follow superstitious customs. The intransigent parliamentarians denounced the audacity of this supplication and the reaffirmation of the Vaudois' articles of faith. The king granted another three-month delay and the Parliament sent the bishop of Cavaillon to Mérindol to receive their abjuration on the spot. After further delays and the refusal of abjuration, the king finally resolved in March 1543 to carry out the order of Mérindol. Once again, German Protestant princes, urged by Farel and Calvin, intervened with the king. The Swiss were a major military power and the king had to reckon with them as well. In April 1544, the Vaudois presented a petition to the king to obtain justice from those who reproached their faith in order to confiscate their possessions. The king was aware of the avarice of the bishops and papal legates, and also knew that the parliamentarians of Aix were not above reproach. He was also hesitant to send military forces to a far-flung province. So he decided to send three members of his council and a theologian to establish whether the Vaudois were heretics. If found to be heretics, they would be granted another two months to abjure. The Parliament of Aix was ordered to relinquish its responsibilities to the Parliament of Grenoble. As a result, the Vaudois sensed that the king hesitated to employ force against them and would defend them from the cupidity of the princes of the Church. Many refugees flocked to the Vaudois valleys to

19. Miquel, *Guerres de religion*, 122–24.

find shelter from persecution. Those in Geneva even thought that they had turned back the royal power. For a time at least![20]

In December 1543 Jean Meynier, Seigneur d'Oppède (1495–1558), replaced Chassané as president of the Parliament of Aix. He had sworn to obtain the revocation of the letters of pardon and to annihilate the Vaudois. The cardinal of Tournon, archbishop of Aix, a declared enemy of heresy agreed. The local governor confirmed the report of Meynier that the Vaudois had a force of ten thousand armed men ready to march on Marseille. The Vaudois, with little confidence in the seigneurs of Aix and Avignon, fortified their villages, notably Cabrières. The king signed an order on January 1, 1545, ostensibly without reading it, revoking the pardon he had granted and persecution in France resumed with burning stakes at Toulouse, Bordeaux, and Grenoble. The cardinal of Tournon introduced the text prepared by Meynier to the council who as lieutenant governor of the king had military powers. Meynier kept the text hidden from his parliamentarian colleagues while awaiting the arrival in Provence of a captain from Italy who the king had named baron, Paulin de La Garde (1498–1578). He was the leader of a fearful band of roving mercenaries who had fought under François I. Once he arrived, the Parliament gave the order to proceed to the total extirpation of the heretics. La Garde marched on Cabrières-d'Aygues where six hundred Vaudois were reportedly gathered. The Vaudois fled and left La Garde wondering why he had been called to employ his army against feeble villagers. At Cadenet, army and parliament leaders from Aix agreed to seize the so-called heretics and burn their houses as an example to others. The brutes of La Garde had not come for no reason; they pillaged and murdered. They were professional soldiers, joined by troops gathered by Meynier and by volunteers eager to profit from the plunder. The inhabitants of Mérindol fled to the Luberon forests while two hundred farms were burned. Hidden in the ravines, the villagers learned that the army had entered Mérindol and watched it burn from a distance. The men mounted upward and joined their brothers in the villages of La Coste and Cabrières-du-Comtat. In the fortified village of Cabrières they decided to stand and resist with three hundred Vaudois combatants. On both sides there were many dead and wounded in the ensuing combat. Led by Marron, the Vaudois did their best but were not equal to the task of resisting against the canons of the enemy. They proposed to open the gates if promised safe passage to Germany or a pledge of fair trials. Promise received, Marron and

20. Miquel, *Guerres de religion*, 124–27.

his partisans exited the village first. They were immediately seized and executed in a nearby meadow. Only Marron and the pastor Guillaume Serre were spared, taken in custody by the pope's legate to Avignon to be judged and burned alive. The female combatants were locked up in a hay loft which was then set ablaze. Those who tried to escape were massacred, their heads carried in triumph on the tips of lances. Soldiers searched for survivors and forced open the door of the church. In the sanctuary women were raped, their throats slit, disemboweled, some thrown from the bell tower. The few women who survived were sold as slaves at L'Isle-sur-le-Sorgue. In one month, nine hundred houses were burned, twenty-four villages destroyed, three thousand people massacred, and six hundred seventy men sent to the galleys. Only the most robust men were spared and sold to spend their remaining days on the king's galley ships.[21]

The galleys appear frequently in the history of the Protestant dissidents from the Vaudois to the Huguenots.[22] We know from history that these floating prisons held men captive in merciless conditions, subject to extremes of heat and cold, weakness and sickness, brutal beatings under the pretext of maintaining discipline, and led to the early death of even the most hardy. Huguenot dogs (*chiens de Huguenots*), one of the many insults hurled against the galley slaves, were considered stubborn and obstinate, and subject to worse treatment than other convicts. For the infraction of refusing to look at the Catholic mass, a cord dipped in pitch was applied to the bare back.[23] In addition, the Parliament made it a crime to provide assistance to those in misery dying from hunger as vagabonds in the fields. Anyone showing pity suffered the confiscation of their possessions. The cavalry of Agoult, installed at the Tour-d'Aigues, roamed throughout the countryside committing atrocities. Peasants were forced to travel to Aix or Marseille to find their kidnapped children and ransom them. The Parliament sent two members to investigate the barbarism and returned horrified. The peasants of Luberon could no longer work their fields without soldiers coming to steal their oxen. The women were robbed in the fields and sometimes left

---

21. Miquel, *Guerres de religion*, 127–33.

22. See *Mémoires d'un galérian du Roi-Soleil* or *Galley Slave* by Jean Marteihe. Condemned to the galleys in 1701 at the age of seventeen, Marteihe's autobiography provides a vivid, eyewitness description of life and death on the galleys under Louis XIV.

23. Whelan, "Enfin libres!" 288–89.

only with a shirt. On the basis of this report the Parliament rendered a new order authorizing the authorities to assist the population.[24]

The king ordered his own investigation and demanded an accounting of the expedition. The cardinal of Tournon supported the cause of Meynier and on August 8, 1545 the king rendered his verdict with approbation of all that was done against the Vaudois to exterminate the sect. Calvin and Farel were devastated by the news and requested an intervention from the Swiss. The king's response and justification to the Swiss was that the Vaudois were disloyal subjects and were punished because they refused to pay the tithe. At the death of François I the tide turned. Meynier sought to continue the persecution and arrested two men with strong connections in Parliament. The cardinal of Tournon was in a state of disgrace with Henri II who designated a commission to investigate Meynier and others involved in the crimes. The indictment against Meynier charged him with deforming the truth about the heretics, undertaking the massacres on his own initiative, and condemning the vagabonds to die of hunger. His eloquence allowed him to save his head and he expressed no remorse for seeking to exterminate the Vaudois. In the end, Meynier d'Oppède was liberated, restored to his functions, and named by the pope chevalier of Saint-Jean-de-Latran. And the Vaudois? Some were able to escape to Geneva where they were well received. Others found refuge in communities in Dauphiné. In any case, they powerfully aided the Reformed cause in gaining a foothold in the Cévennes and Languedoc.[25] Several years later, Sébastian Castellion (1515–1564), who ministered alongside Calvin for a time in Geneva, wrote in the preface to his *Traité des hérétiques*, "Who would want to become a Christian when they see that those who confess the name of Christ are bruised at the hands of Christians, by fire, by water, by sword, and treated more cruelly than robbers and murderers?"[26]

---

24. Miquel, *Guerres de religion*, 133.

25. Miquel, *Guerres de religion*, 134–35.

26. Delumeau, *Le christianisme*, 81.

Chapter 4

Prelude to Wars of Religion

FOR FORTY-THREE YEARS, FROM the entrance of Bishop Briçonnet at Meaux in 1516 until the accidental jousting-related death of Henri II in 1559 which swept the house of Guise to power, the Reformation developed in a kingdom constantly at war under kings who either hesitated or lacked the means to totally root out heresy. A new faith was revealed, accompanied by confusion at times, then reinforced and defined during half a century of intermittent persecutions. In time the evangelicalism of Lefèvre d'Étaples was transformed into Calvinism. What remained of the primitive beginnings was the love of the gospel and the desire to strip unbiblical trappings from the faith. Around 1540 the expression *"les hérésies pullulent"* (heresies swarm) appeared with increasing frequency in royal edicts and parliamentary declarations and evidenced the mounting concern and powerlessness to stop the rising tide of Protestant heresy. Reformed believers, of course, did not think of themselves as heretics but considered themselves loyal subjects of the king.[1]

The framework of Reformed churches suited the French social fabric particularly in villages where people wanted a pastor who preached, celebrated the Lord's Supper, baptized, and officiated at funerals. Many were drawn by the simplicity of the new confession. The role of women was critical in the diffusion of the Reformation and in the organization of churches. The persecution and the resistance of the Huguenots after the affair of the placards in 1534, however, had transformed and hardened the mentalities. Certainly the king was not about to change his opinion about

---

1. Garrisson, *Histoire des protestants*, 43.

the prominence of the Catholic Church. There would be trials and a period of resistance without violence, for Calvin had forbidden and condemned revolution. During this long period of clandestinity, connections were woven patiently in universities and monasteries among those who dreamed of another Church, of another way of life. Persecution prevented many from declaring their faith publicly; many others were obligated to retract or abandon their confession. Yet the victory of Calvinism at Geneva gave the movement cohesion, an appearance of organization, and significant growth in France. At François I's death this clandestine movement was in place.[2]

The first Reformed churches appeared in France in 1555. In 1559 a national synod gathered in Paris and adopted a confession of faith which was ratified in 1571 at La Rochelle and called the *La Confession de la Rochelle*.[3] By 1562 Calvinism became a considerable power in the kingdom with an estimated two million adherents. Among them were academics and former religious workers, legal and commercial professionals, and representatives of high and low nobility, whose conversions led to the conversion of entire cities and villages.[4] This Protestant religious expression "threatened the perception of nation forged by both king and subjects, because the king's own coronation oath required him to protect and defend his realm and his subjects from heresy."[5] Those belonging to the traditional and majority religion refused to accept those of another religious confession. The growth of this new faith raised fears and concerns that needed to be addressed by the royal family since the converts to Protestantism "were simply too numerous to suppress."[6] We have seen early repression beginning in the 1520s, and by the 1540s persecution became practically systematic with many Protestants dying at the stake. Their strength and determination frightened the Catholic hierarchy and constrained the authorities to seek a solution.[7] The house of Guise stood ready to defend the honor and supremacy of the Catholic religion, the unity of the Church and Crown, and to crush the Protestant uprising.

2. Miquel, *Guerres de religion*, 201–2.

3. Carbonnier-Burkard, *La révolte des* Camisards, 10.

4. De Montclos, *Histoire religieuse*, 60.

5. Holt, "Kingdom of France," 23.

6. Holt, "Kingdom of France," 25.

7. De Montclos, *Histoire religieuse*, 60.

HOUSE OF GUISE AND FRANÇOIS II

The house of Guise came to power after the accidental death of Henri II in 1559 and the short reign of his young son François II (1544–1560). After the death of Henri II, Protestants had hoped to obtain the end of repressive measures against them. His successor, during the seventeen months he reigned, turned over the reins of power to the Guises, the uncles of his wife, Mary Stuart, Queen of Scotland. The queen mother, Catherine de Médicis, had advised François II to appoint the Guises as ministers. François de Guise was the second Duke of Guise after his father Claude, who had married Antoinette de Bourbon and become related to the royal family. François was a national military hero with exploits at Calais and Metz. His brother Charles, cardinal of Lorraine (1524–1574), had already been appointed master of the royal council under Henri II. François de Guise was appointed lieutenant-general of the king's armies, married Anne d'Este, granddaughter of Louis XII, and possessed vast land holdings and enormous wealth.[8]

Members of the houses of Bourbon-Vendôme and Bourbon-Montpensier, with royal bloodlines (*princes du sang*), who by birth were closer to the throne, were sidelined by the house of Guise. The royal princes were the fickle Antoine de Bourbon (1518–1562), who through marriage to Jeanne d'Albret (1528–1572), daughter of Marguerite de Navarre, became king of Navarre; Cardinal Charles de Bourbon (1523–1590); and Louis de Bourbon, prince of Condé. The latter, through his marriage to Eléonore de Roy, was sympathetic to Calvinists. An earlier act of treason in 1523 by Charles III de Bourbon (1490–1527), constable of France under François I, weighed heavily on the house of Bourbon with their loyalty to the Crown in question. As a result, both François I and Henri II favored nobles and outsiders to command the armies and to occupy important positions of the crown. These circumstances led Reformed believers to see the royal princes, enemies of the Guises, as their potential protectors. Yet the Bourbon princes were powerless to oppose the Guises who had the support of Philip II of Spain, who promised forty thousand men if the *princes du sang* led a rebellion.[9]

The Guises were partisans of a policy of fierce opposition toward the Reformed religion. Persecution began in a spectacular way with the

8. Miquel, *Guerres de religion*, 205–6.
9. Miquel, *Guerres de religion*, 206–8.

execution in December 1559 of Anne du Bourg (1521–1559), a distinguished member of Parliament. The parliamentarian was declared a heretic by the episcopal tribunal of Paris. After exhausting all his appeals, he was condemned by the archbishops of Sens and Lyon and delivered to the secular authorities to burn at the stake at the Place de Grève, now known as the Place de l'Hôtel de Ville in Paris. He was accorded the grace of strangulation before feeling the flame. There had been other pyres burning in Paris but this one took on symbolic value. Anne du Bourg was a member of Parliament who had dared to defy the deceased king Henri II. His execution manifested the intention of the monarchy to arbitrarily impose its will without taking into account the tremendous expansion of the Reformed movement in the kingdom. More than ever, the royal government demonstrated through a rigorous policy that there would be no sharing of power, and that the ruling authority would remain exclusively Catholic.[10]

A failed Protestant conspiracy to kidnap François II at Amboise in March 1560 to remove him from the influence of the Guises hardened the Guises' resolve to rid the kingdom of heretics. Although this kidnapping attempt was a fiasco, it signaled the bloody dawn of the Huguenot struggle for freedom of conscience. A crucial distinction was now made between dissidence and sedition.[11] Antoine de Bourbon and Louis de Bourbon, wronged and deprived of their rights, belonged to the group of conspirators. The Guises had a vast network of spies and as troops of La Renaudie advanced silently toward the sovereign's residence the trap was sprung. Small groups of conspirators were hunted and killed, some hanged from the gates of the chateau as an example. Several months later, Louis de Condé was arrested and imprisoned at Orléans as the head of the conspiracy. The death of François II allowed him to escape the sentence of death pronounced against him.[12]

The persecution resumed with houses searched in Saint-Germain, known as "Little Geneva." Protestant homes in Paris were located and the arrests and denunciations accelerated. At Villers-Cottêrets, the Guises had the king sign a declaration to purge cities of Protestant houses where assemblies for prayer and the Lord's Supper were secretly held. Statues of the Virgin were placed at intersections throughout Paris to collect offerings at the foot of the statues from passersby. Those who gave nothing betrayed

---

10. Miquel, *Guerres de religion*, 208–9.

11. Foa, "Les droits fragiles," 95.

12. Garrisson, *Histoire des protestants*, 106–7.

themselves as heretics and were beaten. Collections were made house-to-house and those who refused a contribution had their homes plundered. Understandably, not all Reformed believers in Paris were ready to become martyrs. The police profited from their fear and weakness to obtain addresses of other suspected heretics which resulted in many arrests. Fanaticized by sermons, Catholics hunted down the suspects and multiplied the violence. Not all Protestants, however, shrank back in the face of provocation. On Christmas night, a group of Huguenots killed a priest in a suburb of Paris at the moment when he elevated the host. Catholics surrounded the church and massacred the assassins. From that time on, the Huguenots no longer passively suffered persecution and organized themselves for their defense. The escalation of violence and reprisals opened the way for excesses from both camps. The violence was now practiced not only by exuberant fanatics but by professionals of warfare. France was experiencing a period of peace from foreign wars and many soldiers dismissed from the armies no longer had the wherewithal to survive. Those who had an inclination for the ideas of the new confession allied themselves with churches to provide armed resistance. Others sold themselves to the bourgeois to defend their property. The Guises now dreaded civil war as much as they feared Reformed adherents.[13]

COUNCIL OF TRENT (1545–1563)

Before looking at the interminable wars of the last half of the sixteenth century, we should understand how the Catholic Church sought to defend herself against schism and retain her position. The corruption of the Church and the need for reform was undeniable. The Reformation had been welcomed in large part because of the simplicity and clarity of the gospel. For many, the established religion had become mere ritual, human tradition, and superstition. The popes had become earthly princes rather than spiritual leaders and they hesitated to call a council to address the deplorable state of the Church and the priesthood. They had not understood the power and the reach of the Reformation and did not have the courage and conviction to work for the profound renewal needed. Any council initiatives were further frustrated and complicated "by the tussle between

---

13. Miquel, *Guerres de religion*, 209–10.

the imperial demand for reforming decrees and the papal preference for doctrinal decrees."[14]

The constant state of war between François I and Charles V had interfered with attempts to hold a council to address the Protestant heresy. In 1522 many had placed their hope in Pope Adrian VI (1459–1523) to undertake reform. He died nine months after his election. Clement VII (1478–1534), called the most miserable of popes, had seen the sack of Rome and the birth of the Anglican Church. He refused to convene a council. The council was finally gathered at Trent in 1545 under Pope Paul III (1468–1549) who did not live to see it to the end. But it was too late to stop the schism. The Lutheran Church had organized in Germany, England had broken with the papacy, and Calvinism had spread throughout France. The work of the Council of Trent continued with many interruptions until 1563. There was conflict between the nobility and Rome. The princes were divided among themselves but wanted to see religious peace and were hostile toward papal pretensions of authority. Pope Paul III distrusted Charles V and insisted the council take place in an Italian city. Three sessions took place at Bologna before the council ended in 1549. The council recommenced under Pope Julius III (1487–1555) for five sessions from May 1551 to August 1552. Henri II, politically favoring Gallicanism and dreaming of a patriarchy in France, refused to participate and instead sent an observer. After the brief pontificate of Marcellus II in April 1555, the irascible and impulsive Pope Paul IV (1476–1559) sought pretexts to adjourn the council which led to long delays. The council gathered again from January 1562 to December 1563. Pope Pius IV (1499–1565) fearing that France might convene a national council, finally resolved to restart sessions which were marked by divisions between Spain and Italy and which contributed to the triumph of the papacy. Catherine de Médicis and the emperor both had proposed, in vain, that both elements be received in communion and supported the marriage of priests. And French bishops failed to have the council accept any proposition favorable to Gallican liberties.[15]

The final decisions of the Council of Trent demonstrate that the Catholic Church had no intention of healing the rupture between the two confessions, of returning to the gospel, or of making doctrinal concessions. The council's decrees "embodied the victory of the most anti-Protestant point of view" and "the Lutheran tenet that justification comes by faith

14. Elton, *Reformation Europe*, 136.

15. Stéphan, *L'Épopée huguenote*, 114–15.

alone (*sola fide*) was expressly denied."[16] The Church was obsessed with
standing against freedom of conscience, establishing her authority, and
strengthening her unity. The pope was declared the "universal pastor of
the Church" with full authority over the universal Church and the only
interpreter of Scriptures and, contrary to the Council of Constance (1414–
1418), declared superior to councils. The council affirmed that the doctrine
of the Catholic Church was founded on the Scriptures completed by traditions. The Church maintained the seven sacraments purportedly instituted
by Christ, the Vulgate as the orthodox text of the Bible, the real presence
of Christ in the Eucharist, purgatory, salvation by works, indulgences, and
veneration of saints and images. The traditional liturgy with Latin as the
language of the Church was preserved in order to assure the unity of worship among diverse nations and languages. Concerning discipline in the
Church, the celibacy of priests was maintained, priests and bishops were
required to reside in their parishes, and the age for priests and bishops was
established, twenty-five and thirty years old, respectively. The council endeavored to establish a seriousness and dignity for the clergy. Venice, other
Italian states, Poland and Portugal completely accepted the decrees while
Spain and France had reservations. The French Gallican church did not
accept that bishops accused of heresy would be tried before a pontifical
tribunal that did not include the king. By 1615 the decrees were accepted,
at least on the surface, by the national assembly of French clergy, although
under Louis XIV the struggle between the monarchy and the Holy See
would continue.[17]

The Council of Trent led to a great Catholic renaissance under future
popes, Pius V (1504–1572), Gregory XIII (1502–1585), Sixtus V (1521–
1590), and Clement VIII (1536–1605). Schools were established, missions
developed, churches constructed or restored, and new monastic orders
formed. The Jesuits, the Society of Jesus, founded by Ignatius of Loyola
(1491–1556) in 1537 initially faced hostility from the French Parliament
attached to Gallican liberties and saw the Jesuits as a foreign order. Yet the
Jesuits succeeded in infiltrating schools and influencing students. Their first
scholastic establishment at Clermont was recognized by the Parliament in
1562. Although expelled from England in 1583, barred from France in
1594 after an assassination attempt against Henri IV, and ejected from Venice in 1606, these times of exile were temporary and during the seventeenth

16. Elton, *Reformation Europe*, 137.

17. Stéphan, *L'Épopée huguenote*, 116–17.

and eighteenth century they took control of two hundred schools. In the seventeenth century they became the most cunning and relentless enemies of Protestantism.[18]

CATHERINE DE MÉDICIS

At the death of François II in December 1560, Catherine de Médicis (1519–1589), widow of Henri II and niece of Pope Clement VII, became queen of France and ten-year old Charles IX (1550–1574) was proclaimed king. When she arrived in power, Reformed believers enjoyed no religious rights. The Edict of Écouen, signed by Henri II one month before his death on June 2, 1559, made Protestant heresy a crime tried by civil judges. Catherine considered repression a failure and believed that martyrdom had engendered proselytes. The gallows and stakes provided a platform for the condemned and gave evidence of their love for and allegiance to God.[19] The queen maneuvered between three powerful families—Guise, Montmorency, and Bourbon. Louis de Bourbon, prince of Condé, who earlier had escaped a death sentence, returned to the court, and Antoine de Bourbon was appointed head of the armies. The Guises were enraged by this turn of events and by concessions made to the Huguenots but were no longer masters of the kingdom. Catherine showed favor toward Reformed believers which according to some estimates numbered a quarter of the population.[20] She wrote to Pope Pius IV to explain that it was impossible to rid the kingdom of Protestants by weapons or laws, and informed him that French Protestants held no Anabaptist or anti-trinitarian teachings. Among her requests, she asked that the Pope remove the worship of images, that communicants receive both elements in communion, and that the faithful be allowed to sing Psalms in their own language. The pope, who had been solicited by Emperor Ferdinand (1503–1564) in a similar sense, was not disposed to accept these radical measures.[21]

At Paris, the populace remained largely faithful to the Church while Protestants in the provinces understood Catherine's tolerance as tacit approval to gather publicly for worship. From 1558 to 1562 there was a marked

18. Stéphan, *L'Épopée huguenote*, 126–27.

19. Foa, "Les droits fragiles," 94.

20. Estimates for the number of Protestants in 1560 vary widely. Foa in "Les droits fragiles," estimates ten percent of the king's subjects were Protestant in 1560 (93).

21. Stéphan, *L'Épopée huguenote*, 99–101.

change in the social makeup of Protestants. Many among the nobility and the bourgeois were won over to the Protestant cause. The gathering of the Estates General[22] at Orléans in 1560 "saw an open alliance of the nobles and bourgeois in what appears to have been a Calvinist-inspired attack on the privileges and wealth of the church" which ensured that "the Wars of Religion would not be primarily a class conflict, but rather the clash of two rival aristocratic-led factions."[23] Throughout many regions Protestants gathered openly with military protection from nobles. At Rouen, in Normandy and in Cotentin, the faithful were summoned to worship by church bells without facing indignation from Catholics. Calvin, for his part, expressed concern over this exhilaration of freedom and feared it might be taken as provocation. He was right. By early 1561 Catholics became outraged as Protestants held processions in cities and gathered in public squares with armed guards. Several churches in Montpellier and Montauban were seized by Protestants. At Meaux a church building was bought from the bishop. Fanatics chased priests and worshippers from churches in Languedoc and Guyenne. In Dauphiné, armed groups forcibly entered churches, broke statues and forbade entry to Catholics to worship. Catholics throughout the country vehemently protested against the leniency of the queen. They also learned that the queen allowed Admiral Gaspard de Coligny (1519–1572) and the royal princes to use their residences as places of worship. It was even reported that Coligny had invited preachers from Geneva. The freedom accorded to Reformed believers was seen as scandalous and weakening the Crown.[24]

The spectacular conversion of Jeanne d'Albret, queen of Navarre, under the influence of Theodore Beza, whose conversion contrasted with the irresolution of her husband, Antoine de Bourbon, brought a political response to growing calls for repression of the Protestant movement. She was a remarkable woman who had planned and inspected the fortifications at Béarn when the Spanish mobilized at the borders. At Christmas in 1560, Jeanne d'Albret publicly took part in an observation of the Lord's Supper. She had written to Calvin and requested that he persuade her husband to follow her example. On her voyage to Paris in 1561 to meet Catherine de Médicis, she stopped along the way at Limoges, Tours, and cities of the

22. The Estates General (*les états généraux*) were assemblies convened by the king to provide counsel or vote on subsidies (*Nouveau Petit Robert*, 942).

23. McGrath, *John Calvin*, 190.

24. Miquel, *Guerres de religion*, 219–23.

Loire Valley, and frequented places of worship. She was justly called by her biographer Yves Cazaux the queen of the Reformation. Upon her arrival in Paris, fifteen thousand Protestants waited for her with enthusiasm. She was received as a queen with grand ceremony, fireworks displays, and escorted by her husband and nobles. Her intention was to make an impression on public opinion and show the strength of her religion.[25]

Catherine de Médicis understood the growing influence and power of Protestantism and sought to succeed in achieving an accord with the Calvinists where Charles V had failed with the Lutherans. To this end, she decided to gather a national synod in September 1561 at Poissy where Protestant leaders were invited before the king, the royal court, and prelates. The delegation had ten pastors and twenty-two lay leaders led by Theodore Beza, sent in Calvin's place. After speeches from the king and chancellor, the delegates of the Reformed churches were introduced as in a courtroom. Theodore Beza eloquently expounded Calvinist doctrine without avoiding the thorny question of the Eucharist. He explained that although Jesus Christ is not absent from the Lord's Supper, he is not corporally present. There was a collective groan from the bishops. The cardinal of Tournon accused him of blasphemy and implored Catherine to not give any credence to this teaching. Her response was that she and the king would die in the Catholic faith. At a session several days later the cardinal of Lorraine defended the scholastic authority of the Church and the real presence of Christ in the Eucharist. An agreement seemed impossible, with the two parties unable to agree on even a vague confession of faith. The Jesuits, who had recently obtained the authorization to establish themselves in France, benefited greatly from this failed exchange in spite of the hostility of the Gallican wing of the French Church. Diego Lainez (1512–1565), Loyola's second in command, reproached the queen for dealing with excommunicated persons and manifested his violence toward the Huguenots, treating them as wolves, foxes, and assassins. He further insisted that questions of faith were not decided by nations but by the Council of Trent and contended that the faith could not be discussed, only imposed. The colloquium at Poissy showed the impossibility of unity for these two confessions. In spite of disagreements, the Chancellor Michel de l'Hôpital believed it was still possible for adherents of the two confessions to live side by side in

25. Miquel, *Guerres de religion*, 223–24.

peace as citizens notwithstanding their religious commitments. He would soon be proven wrong.[26]

EDICT OF JANUARY

Michel de l'Hôpital was named chancellor by Catherine de Médicis on April 1, 1560. He formulated a theory dissociating citizenship and religion and urged acceptance of those of the new religion. Subsequent edicts amplified this distinction partly due to the strength of Protestantism in southern France and the growing impossibility of denying Protestant interests and influence. Although only Catholics could hold public processions, Protestants, still deprived of rights in public space, experienced tolerance in their private exercise of freedom of conscience and their homes were no longer searched. Through an edict in July 1561 the monarchy ordered the liberation of all religious prisoners. On January 17, 1562, Catherine de Médicis' Edict of January accorded the Huguenots limited rights for private religious practices in government- approved places. The terms "heresy" and "heretics" were removed from royal legislation and Protestants obtained complete freedom of conscience with limited freedom of worship.[27] Large religious gatherings were still forbidden in population centers where the Huguenots were concentrated, Catholic churches they had occupied needed to be restituted, and they were forbidden to destroy images or crosses.[28] Yet according to Lindberg, "Huguenot public worship was allowed in private homes in towns and outside the towns' walls. This was the watershed for French Protestantism."[29]

The Edict of January came about after earlier events made royal concessions necessary. Certainly, violence had played an important role in obtaining these rights. The Huguenots had taken up arms and seized the cities of Rouen, Lyon, and Montpellier. Even more importantly, letters and petitions were addressed to the Crown by Reformed believers to request relief. After the failed attempt to kidnap François II in 1560, the monarch conceded to Protestants an essential right—the right of petition. This was the first right historically granted to Protestants: the right of access to the king as good and loyal subjects. From a political and legal point of view, the right

26. Stéphan, *L'Épopée huguenote*, 101–2.

27. Foa, "Les droits fragiles," 96.

28. Stéphan, *L'Épopée huguenote*, 103.

29. Lindberg, *European Reformation*, 289.

to petition was revolutionary. Other rights were implicitly recognized—the right to refuse immediate and forced conversion to Catholicism, the right to call assemblies, and the right of safe passage to present petitions to the king. Petitions multiplied between Huguenots and the Crown with the principal objective the legal recognition and protection of the Protestant minority and to be treated equally with Catholics under the law.[30]

The Edict of January was rejected by most French Catholics who raised the question, "How could the regent, wife, and mother of a king of France advocate the Huguenots' legal right to exist within the kingdom, when the king's own coronation required their suppression?"[31] The authorities of the Church considered Catherine's edict in contradiction to the Council of Trent which had anathematized the heresy of Luther and Calvin. She soon became aware of the dangerous situation in which the edict placed her and sought to side with and placate the Catholic faction. War seemed inevitable. "The Huguenot political and military resources were not sufficient to bring France into Protestantism, but they were strong enough to ensure their existence as a rebellious minority."[32] Yet the Edict of January had broken with the past and "made France the first Western European kingdom to grant legal recognition to two forms of Christianity at once."[33]

By the very nature of edicts at the time, however, these rights remained fragile, subject to the political winds of ruling powers and revocable. The Edict of January was dated with a provisional seal. Later, beginning with the Edict of Saint-Germain in 1570, edicts were sealed with green wax and contained the clause "perpetual and irrevocable." This clause will be found in future edicts, including the Edict of Nantes in 1598 which in reality was neither perpetual nor irrevocable. In fact, several times during the Wars of Religion, notably with the Edict of Saint-Maur (September 1568) followed by the Edict of Nemours (July 1585), the Huguenots saw their rights suddenly revoked with a call to convert to Catholicism. In a few hours, all was lost—houses, places of worship, even cities. At the outbreak of each new conflict, their rights were challenged, often by the very prince who had granted them. Subjects of the State, they were subjected by the same State to decrees of expulsion, pillage, and massacres. They soon learned that what had been granted by the good graces of the king might be revoked by his

30. Foa, "Les droits fragiles," 96–98.

31. Holt, "Kingdom of France," 25.

32. Lindberg, *European Reformation*, 290.

33. Benedict, "Wars of Religion," 147.

good pleasure. With the Edict of Saint-Maur, Huguenot officers were re-moved from their posts. Hundreds, indeed, thousands of Reformed officers experienced a lack of confidence in the word of the State. While those in other occupations suffered, military officers lost their prized titles and were unable to exercise their profession. Wounded in their pride and relieved from their prestigious positions, many of these officers would soon be on the fields of battle during the Wars of Religion.[34]

34. Foa, "Les droits fragiles," 100–103.

Chapter 5

Wars of Religion

THE WARS OF RELIGION first broke out in the spring of 1562 and would last for over three decades. These wars "made clear that France was divided—regionally, socially, and politically—by Calvinism."[1] During these wars there were three periods where the Huguenots wrestled with the dilemma of obedience to the king and obedience to God. The first period dates from the conspiracy of Amboise to kidnap François II in 1560 to Saint Bartholomew in 1572 when the Huguenots endeavored to reconcile their obedience to the king and their obedience to God. They recognized the teachings of Calvin concerning obedience to authority and their duty to honor the king, but the legitimacy of the conspiracy was questioned by Calvin since it was conducted by private individuals rather than by legitimate authority. The second period followed the Saint Bartholomew's Day massacre at which time their position grew more radical in retaliation for the slaughter of Huguenots throughout France and reflected their duty to resist unjust rulers. Some historians point to Calvin's evolving thinking and ambiguity on active resistance to tyranny as justification for Huguenot acts of resistance and retaliation during this time. This period coincided with the rise of the *Monarchomaque* movement which held to a monarchy by contractual agreement, conditional obedience, and was a precursor to the constitutional monarchy.[2] The final period was opened by the death of François d'Alençon (*Monsieur*), the last brother of Henri III which placed

1. McGrath, *John Calvin*, 193.
2. Engammare, "Calvin monarchomaque? Du soupçon à l'argument," 207.

51

Henri de Navarre in direct line of succession, in which the Huguenots sought to resolve the conflict tearing at their consciences.[3]

The Reformation had reached it numerical peak in 1560, and the following years would see the numbers ebb. Beginning in 1560, two years before the wars commenced, lists of Huguenots were created in many cities to deprive people of their rights. One's name on the list meant running the risk of losing all rights each time a conflict broke out. Throughout these times of trouble, cities used these lists to banish Protestants. Constituted in times of peace, often with the complicity of one's neighbors, these lists lay dormant for a few months or a few years until needed in time of war to exile Huguenots and claim their homes and all they contained. Their rights were ephemeral, their possessions lost overnight, their communities destroyed, and their future compromised.[4] They took up arms to defend themselves, their families, and their religion. They were often used as pawns for political purposes. They lost all confidence in the stability of a world collapsing around them and in the frayed institutions of their nation. Those who rebuffed intimidating attempts to convert them to Catholicism, or refused the supreme allegiance to a monarch owed to God alone, had no other option than to resist. Eight wars took place interspersed with brief periods of peace and compromises, finally ending with the war of three Henris between dynastic rivalries—King Henri III, also known as Henri de Valois and earlier as Duke of Anjou; Henri de Lorraine (1550–1588), Duke of Guise; and Henri de Bourbon, Huguenot leader and king of Navarre, the future King Henri IV. During the Wars of Religion, "so frequent and gruesome were the massacres accompanying these conflicts, so searing the sieges, and so numerous the assassinations of leading political actors, that the events of the 'time of religious troubles' burned themselves into French and European historical memory for centuries to come."[5]

FIRST WAR OF RELIGION (1562–1563)

The massacre of Protestants in Vassy in Champagne in March 1562 foreshadowed the bloodshed which would follow in the Wars of Religion. At stake was the status of the Reformed religion in the kingdom.[6] The

3. Daussy, "Entre l'obéisance au roi et l'obéissance à Dieu," 49–50.
4. Foa, "Les droits fragiles," 104–5.
5. Benedict, "Wars of Religion," 147.
6. Carbonnier-Burkard, La révolte des Camisards, 14–15.

power-hungry house of Guise was at the center of intrigues and attempts to rid the kingdom of Huguenots. François de Guise engaged in subterfuge with German Lutherans and pretended to be favorable toward the Confession of Augsburg in order to separate Lutherans from French Protestants. His mother, Antoinette de Bourbon, shared her son's antipathy toward the Huguenots and was displeased to see the spread of Calvinism in the region. On Sunday, March 1 the duke learned that over five hundred Huguenots were meeting in a barn at a time when Reformed worship was forbidden in cities under the stipulations of the Edict of January. With two hundred armed men, he came across this large congregation of Huguenots gathered at a short distance from the Catholic Church and attacked them. Accounts of the number of victims vary. Stéphan writes of twenty-three dead and one hundred wounded. Others claim some seventy Huguenots, men, women, and children were massacred and many more wounded. In any case, the incident sparked more massacres, and the religious wars were on. The duke was received in Paris with a triumphal entry and Catholics compared him to Judas Maccabees as the defender of the faith.[7] The impassioned anti-Protestant crowd and the reaction of the authorities prompted leading Huguenot nobles to capture cities. Throughout the first war of religion, the seizure of cities became high stakes for the two camps. Several cities, quickly acquired in April and May 1562 were soon lost by the Protestants—Rouen, Tours, Blois, Sens, Angers, and Beaugency. Other cities would be held longer—Grenoble, Lyon, Gaillac, and Valence. Finally, some cities, thanks to a religious consensus remained Calvinist until 1598—Nîmes, Montauban, La Rochelle, La Charité-sur Loire, Sancerre, Nérac, Lectoure, and Castres.[8]

With the Edict of January the Huguenots felt they had almost obtained freedom of conscience, but soon they were confronted by violations of the edict. Following the massacre at Vassy, Protestant forces seized cities in which they reportedly destroyed Catholic churches and sacred relics considered part of idolatrous practices.[9] At Tours, two hundred Huguenots were slain with their bodies tossed into the Loire River. At Sens, Protestants were slaughtered and their bodies thrown into the Yonne River with the cadavers floating to Paris. The Huguenots responded by killing priests and monks, sacking churches, and melting down chalices and bells. In excesses

---

7. Stéphan, *L'Épopée huguenote*, 107.

8. Garrisson, *Histoire des protestants,* 107–8.

9. Nelson, "Remembering the Martyrdom," 76.

of rage, sepulchers were destroyed and the Huguenots became more intractable as massacres spread.[10]

In July, Parliament declared that Protestants were outlaws. The war spread throughout Provence, Dauphiné, Languedoc, and Condé captured Orléans, Angers, Tours, and Blois. Lyon fell soon afterwards. Huguenot leaders negotiated the Treaty of Hampton-Court on September 20, 1562 with Queen Elizabeth I (1533–1603) of England to provide funds and six thousand soldiers with the condition that Le Havre be given her as a pledge until the city of Calais, granted to England by the Treaty of Cateau-Cambrésis in 1559, was returned to English control. Three Catholic *grands seigneurs*, the Constable de Montmorency, Jacques d'Albon, and François de Guise, known as the Triumvirate (*triumvirs*), united themselves against the Protestants. They attempted to retake Rouen before the debarkation of English troops and Catherine de Médicis arrived to rally the besiegers. The siege lasted for five weeks, the city fell on October 26, 1562, and was sacked and pillaged. Antoine de Bourbon was mortally wounded and died shortly after. After the fall of Rouen, the Huguenots marched toward Normandy with reinforcements and were attacked by the Catholics at Dreux. The battle lasted seven hours and ended with the Duke of Guise victorious and the capture of Condé. Admiral Coligny, now the leader of the Huguenot army, left his brother François d'Andelot (1521–1569) at Orléans and proceeded toward Normandy to rally the English troops. At this point François de Guise attempted to take Orléans only to be shot three times by the Huguenot Poltrot de Méré. The duke died six days later. His family saw the hand of Coligny behind his death and swore to avenge the duke's death. As Coligny took cities in Normandy, Orléans continued its resistance, and a Protestant state began to form in the Midi.[11]

Catherine de Médicis sought peace and engaged Condé, prisoner for the past three months, to negotiate at Orléans. The conditions for peace proposed by the queen were accepted before the arrival of Condé and the Edict of Amboise, also known as the Edict of Pacification, was signed on March 19, 1563. Coligny was furious when he learned of the restrictions of the edict and Calvin accused Condé of betrayal. Provisions of the Edict of January were reversed. The freedom of worship became proportionate to the social condition of Reformed believers. Henceforth, for the common people, freedom of worship was limited to one city per district in private

10. Stéphan, *L'Épopée huguenote*, 129.

11. *Le Midi* designates the region of the south of France (*Nouveau Petit Robert*, 1595).

homes, and greater freedom of worship to assemble was granted to the Protestant nobility and those in cities under their control. As crippling as it was to the Protestant cause, the edict ended several years of armed conflict. Both camps licked their wounds and replaced their dead leaders. The peace was illusory as political and religious passions smoldered under the surface. Catholic fanaticism was rekindled by the return of the Huguenots to a place of favor and here and there the massacres of Huguenots continued.[12]

After the end of hostilities, Queen Elizabeth refused to release Le Havre without the return of Calais and demanded the strict application of the Treaty of Hampton-Court. Coligny and Condé had accepted on good faith that Elizabeth wanted to deliver France from the tyranny of the Guise dynasty and protect Protestants. Negotiations failed with Elizabeth which united Protestants and Catholics in seizing Le Havre from the English in July 1563. Elizabeth finally conceded, received an indemnity, and recognized the definitive French possession of Calais with the Treaty of Troyes on April 11, 1564. Catherine de Médicis benefited greatly from this illusion of peace in consolidating her power. The struggle of the Huguenots continued as provincial parliaments protested the edict of pacification. Catholics found it too generous and the Huguenots considered it humiliating.[13] In this war of extermination, furiously fought by both sides, the Catholics emerged victorious in the sense that the growth of Protestantism stopped in 1563. There would be no peaceful coexistence between two competing religions. In arming themselves against the king's armies, the Huguenots "lost the image of a persecuted church. And when in 1562 they looked to English Protestants for assistance . . . they lost their patriotic credibility."[14]

Beginning in 1564, Catherine de Médicis and an entourage travelled throughout France to showcase the prestige of the monarchy. In her company were the young King Charles IX, his brother Henri d'Orléans, the young prince Henri de Navarre, and Cardinal Charles de Lorraine. At Bayonne, the queen met with the Duke of Albe who requested the expulsion of all Reformed pastors from France and the acceptance of the decisions of the Council of Trent. The negotiations failed and Catherine left after offering vague promises. The voyage continued for about two years during which Catherine observed the loyalty of the population, even among the

12. Garrisson, *Histoire des protestants,* 109–10.

13. Stéphan, *L'Épopée huguenote,* 130–32.

14. Lindberg, *European Reformation,* 290.

Huguenots, and a relative calm.[15] All that would change when King Philip II of Spain sent troops along the French borders to quell a Protestant revolt in Flanders. French Protestants were alarmed in light of the Bayonne meeting and the uncertainty of what decisions or agreements had been made. They suspected a secret agreement decided at Bayonne between Catherine and Philip II. Protestant military leaders François d'Andelot and Louis de Condé no longer commanded the respect of the Catholic armies they led; the latter was publicly insulted by the sixteen-year old Duke of Anjou who asserted a claim as commander of the armies. More setbacks quickly followed.[16]

SECOND WAR OF RELIGION (1567–1568)

A precarious peace survived for four years following the Edict of Amboise, which suffered multiple violations. Pope Pius V clearly "favored the elimination of the Huguenots, and the outbreak of another round of religious war in September 1567 increased his expectations of success."[17] During this period Catholic Leagues (*ligues catholiques*) were formed for the extirpation of heresy. There were legal processes against Protestants who had pillaged Catholic churches and attacks by organized bands against the minority Protestants. Both sides engaged mercenaries for protection. Certain governors refused to implement the royal decree and threatened the unity of the kingdom. The Huguenots in the Midi, in places where they constituted a majority, found the limitations of the Edict of Amboise unbearable and were determined to resist. In June 1567, Pope Pius V condemned the Huguenots which led Louis de Condé, Gaspard de Coligny, and François d'Andelot to quit the royal court and take up arms once again. Over growing concern of the cardinal of Lorraine's influence on the young King Charles IX, Condé plotted a failed coup to capture the king. The king was informed of the coup and returned to Paris, humiliated, under protection of Swiss guards. The date of this return, September 26, 1567, is considered the beginning of the second war of religion.[18]

    Violence followed with uprisings in various cities and atrocities committed on both sides. The Protestants took their revenge for the humiliation

15. Stéphan, *L'Épopée huguenote*, 133.

16. Miquel, *Guerres de religion*, 259.

17. Martin, "Papal Policy," 45.

18. Stéphan, *L'Épopée huguenote*, 135.

suffered by the Edict of Amboise. Montauban and Orléans returned to Protestant control. At Nîmes, the Huguenot population slaughtered Catholics and their priests on September 30, 1567. Louis de Condé besieged Paris and Huguenots in the city were attacked by Catholics. The royal troops numbering almost twenty thousand under the leadership of Anne de Montmorency left Paris to meet the Huguenot army of five thousand at the battle of Saint Denis on November 10, 1567. The battle was short and indecisive. Anne de Montmorency, wounded, refused to surrender, and escaped with the help of his sons only to die two days later. Reinforcements arrived from foreign countries and the Calvinist prince Frederick III sent ten thousand soldiers which joined up with the army of Coligny. Four thousand troops from southern France joined Condé to besiege the city of Chartres. Italian and Swiss troops reinforced the French king's army but failed to repel the Protestant forces now numbering thirty thousand. Paris was once again besieged. The arrival of winter, the exhaustion of the troops, and the lack of resources led again to negotiation with a treaty signed at Longjumeau on March 23, 1568, which simply reestablished the Edict of Amboise and denied Protestants their request for strongholds. The failure of her policy of religious toleration led Catherine de Médicis to side with the Catholics.[19]

THIRD WAR OF RELIGION (1568–1570)

A brief respite of five months had been obtained in March 1568 with the Edict of Longjumeau. Catholics in the provinces organized into leagues of self-defense to which were added armed brotherhoods. Pope Pius V "supported this new war with every means at his command" and "mounted a diplomatic offensive in order to gain pledges of money and soldiers from other princes."[20] Condé and Coligny found refuge at La Rochelle, a stronghold of Huguenot resistance, led by Jeanne d'Albret and her fifteen-year old son, Henri de Navarre. The third war began and advanced with the international participation of Switzerland, Germany, Italy, and England. Shortly after, Cardinal Charles of Lorraine recovered his position at the head of the royal council. At Toulouse, the king's representative, bearing the Edict of Pacification, was killed. Religious tolerance came to an end with the decree of Saint-Maur in September 1568 which revoked the Edict of Longjumeau. Protestants were forbidden to worship and accused of the

19. Stéphan, *L'Épopée huguenote*, 135–36.
20. Martin, "Papal Policy," 45.

crime of *lèse-majesté*. At Paris, King Charles IX, the *roi très chrétien*, organized a spectacular manifestation to publicly declare his defense of Catholicism. The civil war in France was also influenced by international events, in
particular the revolt and the repression of the subjects of Philip II in Holland which aroused emotions in France. Each side benefited from foreign
assistance; the Catholics from King Philip II of Spain, Pope Pius V, and the
Duke of Tuscany; the Protestants from William of Nassau, Duke of Orange
with whom Condé and Coligny signed an alliance, and from Elizabeth of
England who financed expeditions in France.[21]

Catholic forces marked two notable victories, at Jarnac in March 1569
and at Moncontour in October 1569. At Jarnac, the Duke of Anjou, future
Henri III, defeated Condé, who after falling from his horse and breaking his
leg, was executed at the moment of surrender with a bullet in the head. The
order was given to slit the throats of the Huguenot leaders. Coligny escaped
and rejoined Jeanne d'Albret who presented her son Henri de Navarre and
Henri I de Bourbon, the son of Louis de Condé, to the troops as their new
military leaders. Thanks to German reinforcements, Coligny defeated the
forces of the Duke of Anjou at the Roche-Abeille in June 1569. At Montcon-
tour, however, twenty-seven thousand royal troops and Swiss mercenaries
inflicted a serious defeat on the Huguenots who numbered sixteen thousand. All the prisoners were killed. Coligny, seriously wounded, escaped
and headed north toward La Charité-sur-Loire where the Protestants won
the battle of Arnay-le-Duc on June 27, 1570. With Paris now threatened,
Catherine de Médicis requested a suspension of combat. The cardinal of
Lorraine left the royal court and the Peace of Saint-Germain was signed on
August 8, 1570. The third war of religion ended. With the Edict of Saint-
Germain, the Protestants obtained a temporary reprieve from their troubles. The edict guaranteed freedom of conscience and freedom of worship
in designated locales. Four cities were guaranteed protection—La Rochelle,
Cognac, Montauban, and La Charité-sur Loire—and kept their garrisons.
The royal power prudently recognized the need to tread carefully with a
powerful minority. An appearance of tranquility reigned in France with
a semblance of peaceful coexistence. The peace was short-lived, criticized
by the Pope, and unacceptable to Catholics with the loss of four cities no
longer under the king's authority.[22]

---

21. Miquel, *Guerres de religion*, 267.

22. Stéphan, *L'Épopée huguenote*, 136–37; Miquel, *Guerres de religion*, 268.

FOURTH WAR OF RELIGION (1572–1573)

With Reformed believers reestablished in the public life of the kingdom, Catherine de Médicis drew closer to Reformed leaders and began to arrange marriages. After all, she had seven children to marry off and they were often connected to her intrigues. After having married her son Charles IX to Elisabeth d'Autriche, she plotted to marry her favorite son Henri d'Anjou (1551–1589), later Henri III, to Elizabeth I, Queen of England, and her daughter Marguerite to Henri de Navarre, a Huguenot of the house of Bourbon-Navarre. Coligny returned to the royal court in 1571, held great sway over the young King Charles IX, and pushed him toward an alliance with England and German Protestant princes against Spain. He dreamed of conquering Holland by helping the insurgents in order to make France the most powerful European nation. He also held out hope that a foreign war might reconcile the two religious confessions in France against a common enemy. Charles IX seemed to have adopted Coligny's views without his mother's knowledge. She was concerned about war with Spain but unwilling to align herself with Protestant nations against Catholic powers. It may have been at this time that Catherine, seeing Charles IX enamored with the projects of Coligny, devised a plan to have the admiral assassinated. She waited however for the marriage of her daughter Marguerite with Henri de Navarre.[23] There was surprisingly strong papal opposition to this marriage arrangement. "Instead of viewing the marriage as an opportunity to draw the nominal leader of the Huguenots to the bosom of the Holy Church, Pius viewed it as an enormous threat to Catholicism."[24]

The marriage of Henri de Navarre to Marguerite de Valois took place August 18, 1572 with great pomp. The spectators behind barriers regarded this strange ceremony where the groom did not enter the cathedral to hear the mass and where the couple received the wedding blessing on a raised platform in front of Notre-Dame. The festivities continued until dawn on the twenty-first. On August 22, 1572, an attempt was made on the life of Admiral Gaspard de Coligny returning from the Louvre to his chambers, wounding him on the arm and hand. The house where the would-be assassin had hidden belonged to a partisan of the Guises. Huguenot leaders in Paris for the marriage were outraged and demanded justice.[25] Charles like-

---

23. Stéphan, *L'Épopée huguenote*, 137–38.

24. Martin, "Papal Policy," 47.

25. Garrisson, *Histoire des protestants*, 112.

wise was furious and initially promised punishment for the guilty parties. As a result of this failed assassination, tensions rose among the factions and provided the catalyst for the massacres to follow. Blame for the attempt on Coligny's life has been assigned traditionally to Catherine de Médicis in her attempt to rid her son Charles IX of Coligny's influence, and alternately to Philip II of Spain and the house of Guise as agents of Philip's government. Her role in the attempt on Coligny's life is disputed by historians, although Catherine eagerly welcomed the idea proposed by advisors to murder all the Huguenot leaders, and Charles IX was persuaded of its necessity to avoid a religious war.[26] Municipal leaders were ordered to close the city gates and arm the militia. The Duke of Nevers, Louis Gonzaga, intervened to request that the lives of Henri de Navarre and the prince of Condé be spared.[27] Then the massacre began. Early in the morning on August 24, 1572, a small band of assassins led by the Duke of Guise headed down rue de Béthisy to the inn where Coligny was recovering from his wounds incurred two days earlier. Soldiers ordered by Charles IX to protect the place where Coligny rested joined the band and attacked the inn, murdered Coligny in cold blood, and threw his lifeless corpse out a window.[28] What began as a "controlled operation against the leading Protestant noblemen grew into a vast bloodletting by ardently anti-Protestant members of the civic militia, who had allowed themselves to believe that the king had finally sanctioned the long-hoped-for eradication of all Huguenots."[29] The one-day killing spree turned into a season of slaughter. Three days of massacre followed in Paris where two to three thousand Reformed believers lost their lives. As the news from Paris spread to the provinces, the Catholic populations of Meaux, Orléans, Troyes, Bourges, Samur, and Lyon set upon the Huguenots to exterminate them. French people carried out the bulk of the carnage against Protestants. They slit their throats, dragged them through the streets, threw them into rivers, and as if death were not enough of a punishment, mutilated their cadavers. Catholics looked to the miracle of a dried-out tree in the Holy Innocents' Cemetery which blossomed out of season. Catholic clergy organized a staged production for the miracle. Church bells rang, the guilds paraded by the blooming flowers, women wept, and men convulsed. The purported miracle offered proof that God

26. Martin, "Papal Policy," 35–36.

27. Stéphan, L'Épopée huguenote, 139.

28. De Waele, "Le cadavre du conspirateur," 97.

29. Benedict, "Wars of Religion," 156.

approved the slaughter of the heretics and that the kingdom would once again flourish like the tree as soon as the heresy was eradicated. For simple souls fanaticized by the words of parish priests, Protestants were the scapegoats for all the misfortunes of the times.[30] The Saint Bartholomew's Day massacre relaunched inter-confessional conflict and to this day marks a somber and unforgettable tragedy. Philip II of Spain received the news with great joy. A Catholic historian reports that Pope Gregory XIII (1502–1585), upon receiving the news of the massacre, decreed a jubilee of thanksgiving, struck a commemorative medal, and commissioned Italian artist Vasari to immortalize the event by a fresco on the walls in the Vatican *Sala Regia*.[31]

The massacre provoked a horrified stupor among Protestants and "precipitated a massive wave of defections from the Protestant cause. In the wake of the killing, Charles IX forbade the Reformed believers from gathering for worship—to protect them against violence, his edict proclaimed, but also because he undoubtedly realized that the massacre might end the Protestant problem once and for all."[32] Catherine reaffirmed her domination over the king with the death of Coligny and was flattered by the felicitations of the pope. And when she saw her son-in-law, Henri de Navarre, kneel devoutly before the altar at his conversion to Catholicism and promoted chevalier de Saint-Michel, she judged that the Huguenots had received a mortal blow. Her triumph was only in appearance and Henri's conversion was soon reversed. She was deceived in thinking that the Protestants were finished. Instead they were hardened in their resistance. Great cities like La Rochelle, Montauban, Millau, and Castres closed their gates to royal envoys and Cévenol citadels were transformed into islands of independence. And a good part of Europe expressed disdain for France and especially for her kings.[33] The Saint Bartholomew's Day massacre had not produced its desired effect to rid the kingdom of schismatic Protestants and in the course of time led to "a growing, if still begrudging, acceptance of the argument that religious toleration was less an evil than endless warfare."[34]

La Rochelle was besieged by royal troops under the command of the Duke of Anjou, the future Henri III. As the massacres continued in the provinces for several months, fearful Protestants defected and reembraced

30. Garrisson, *Histoire des protestants,* 113–14.

31. Delumeau, *Le christianisme,* 32.

32. Benedict, "Wars of Religion," 157.

33. Stéphan, *L'Épopée huguenote,* 142.

34. Benedict, "Wars of Religion," 163.

the Catholic religion. Battles raged at Nîmes and Montauban with the cities' refusals to accept royal garrisons. Many fled to find refuge abroad or in Protestant-controlled regions in France. It has been estimated that "Kingdom-wide, for every person killed in the St. Bartholomew's massacres, dozens returned to the Catholic fold or fled abroad."[35] After royal troops failed to conquer La Rochelle, the Edict of Rochelle was signed on July 6, 1573. The edict granted freedom of worship to the cities of La Rochelle, Montauban, and Nîmes, and the freedom of conscience to all Huguenots. The war of men turned to a war of ideas and debates on the legitimacy of the monarchy. The royalty was despised and Charles IX regarded by many as a tyrant. In France and elsewhere, even Catholics were horrified by the bloodshed. A new party formed, the Malcontents, moderate Catholics, who would exploit the brothers of Charles IX against the queen mother, first the Duke of Anjou and then later the Duke of Alençon. In the last year of his reign, Charles IX would see his brother the Duke of Alençon conspire against him, ally himself with the Huguenots, and resist the king's authority. His whole life, Charles IX was nothing more than the servant and instrument of his mother. Two hundred years later the sword would turn against the kings of France. Voilà that which the Saint Bartholomew massacre birthed![36]

FIFTH WAR OF RELIGION (1574–1576)

As soon as Henri III heard of the death of his brother Charles IX, apparently from tuberculosis, he abandoned his throne in Poland and returned to France. His reign was inaugurated with authoritarian measures and he was pressured by his mother Catherine to wage war against the Huguenots. This led to the fifth war of religion. At a general assembly in Millau in August 1574, the Protestants confirmed an agreement with Henri de Montmorency, Duke of Damville (1534–1614), and allied themselves with the Malcontents who desired a regime of religious tolerance. The Malcontents demanded political reform in order to ensure freedom of worship. Protestants in the south of France organized a confederation of provinces. They had lost their confidence in the king and gained assurance in their capacity to resist oppression.[37] They wanted a place in the royal government. The

35. Benedict, "Wars of Religion," 158.
36. Stéphan, *L'Épopée huguenote*, 143–44.
37. Stéphan, *L'Épopée huguenote*, 148.

goal was not an independent State or secession from France. The realities of the time and Catholic threats did not permit the realization of this vision. Catherine, however, found intolerable the questioning of royal authority in the provinces and any consideration of a Protestant State. For her, the kingdom was not a subject of discussion or negotiation.[38]

The fifth war lost some of it religious character in becoming a political war against tyranny. Henri III's brother, François, Duke of Alençon escaped from the court in September 1575 and found refuge in his fief at Dreux. The importance of this event lies in the fact that François was not only of royal blood but next in line for the throne. He allied himself with Condé in southern France, later joined by Henri de Navarre, who had recanted his forced conversion to Catholicism and escaped from the French court. Hostilities also took place in southern provinces under the leadership of Damville. Although Catholic, he allied himself with the Huguenots and proposed to lead the two religions against royal oppression. In October 1575, the Duke of Guise, in his attempt to save the Crown, won a battle against the avant-garde of the army marching toward Paris. The victory was spectacular but not decisive. Catherine sought to make peace with her son, François d'Alençon (1555–1584), and yielded to all his demands in order to save her own crown. The entourage of Henri III, emboldened by the victory of the Duke of Guise, disagreed with Catherine, and Henri III loathed the thought of being humiliated by his brother. Catherine understood that François needed to make the first concession in order to prevent further division among the royal family. Under her influence, he signed a treaty at Champigny which guaranteed a truce among the royals until June 1576. Protestants were granted the freedom of worship in all the cities where they were masters, and several other cities were to be turned over to Protestant control. Many Catholic governors refused to relinquish cities to the Protestants, and German mercenaries assembled in Lorraine scorned the queen's offer to recompense them to cease their military campaign. Henri de Navarre joined the camp of princes and Condé engaged himself to pay the troops with the family jewels. The royal troops of Henri III were no match for the combined forces of his adversaries numbering thirty thousand who set out for Paris. Yet François understood his dilemma as a Catholic leading an army dominated by Protestant princes and hesitated to advance. Condé alone among the princes was determined to press on. After all, for him the war was personal. Burned into his memory was the death of his father,

---

38. Miquel, *Guerres de religion*, 302–3.

killed after surrendering at the Battle of Jarnac in 1569, when Henri III had his body carried unceremoniously on a donkey and exposed to insults in front of a church. Now François, summoned by the other princes, took his place at the front of the army. Panic gripped the court. The order to march on Paris was sufficient for the king to dispatch his mother with a mandate to negotiate. There would be no combat, for now.[39]

An edict of pacification, known as the Edict of Beaulieu, was signed on May 6, 1576. The king took great care to express his regrets for the events of the Saint Bartholomew's Day massacre. Under the edict's terms, Reformed worship was allowed throughout the kingdom except for Paris and immediately surrounding areas. Protestants were permitted access to all employments, accorded eight cities as strongholds under the leadership of Henri I de Bourbon, prince of Condé (1552–1588), and held seats in parliament.[40] In addition, all court proceedings against the Protestants were suspended, seized possessions were restituted, and Protestants were permitted their own cemeteries. Yet Protestants were still obliged to pay the tithe to the Catholic clergy. The Catholic religion was reestablished everywhere and Catholic churches established even in towns under Protestant control. Protestant merchants were required to show respect in closing their business on the days of Catholic festivals and were no longer permitted to sell meat on Friday.[41]

By all measures, the Edict of Beaulieu was by far the most liberal of all the edicts promulgated since the beginning of the Wars of Religion and met most of the demands made earlier by Protestant leaders. In addition, the princes were not forgotten and were generously compensated for losses suffered during these events. Henri de Montmorency received a testimony of affection from the king and remained governor of Languedoc. Henri de Navarre became governor of Guyenne, received authorization from the king to return to his holdings, and was reimbursed for the debts incurred by his mother at the time of his marriage. Condé was named governor of Picardy and given the responsibility, along with Navarre and Damville, for eight fortified cities. To the Duke of Alençon were attributed the provinces of Anjou, Touraine, and Berry in the center of the kingdom. Added to his privileges as heir to the throne, he received the title Duke of Anjou, just as his brother before him. The lords and mercenaries were awarded at the

39. Miquel, *Guerres de religion*, 312–14.

40. Stéphan, *L'Épopée huguenote*, 149.

41. Miquel, *Guerres de religion*, 314–15.

expense and on the backs of the king's subjects. By their excessive claims, the royals and nobles discredited an agreement which for the first time had laid the foundations for true religious peace.[42]

SIXTH WAR OF RELIGION (1577)

The Huguenot victory exasperated the Catholics and embittered the king. Catholic opinion severely judged the Duke of Alençon for accepting the command of Huguenot and foreign forces. The Edict of Beaulieu was derisively called "*la paix de Monsieur*," the brother of the king called "Monsieur" and one of the principal beneficiaries of the edict.[43] In Paris, where the clergy were masters of the population, the Huguenots no longer had any rights. Catholics were furious when they learned of the concessions made to the Huguenots under the edict. The legitimacy was questioned of a king who opened doors for Reformed believers to freely worship and had surrendered cities to Huguenot control. Opposition came from Catholics who borrowed organizational practices from the Huguenots and formed defensive coalitions.[44]

A Catholic League was formed in Normandy in 1576 to oppose Condé. The Duke of Guise, more popular than ever after the battle of Dormans during the fifth war of religion and known for his scarred face, seemed designated to lead the League. The League was not only a religious association to strengthen the grasp of the Catholic church, but a political party attempting to limit royal power. This party had a military organization and elected leaders to whom its members swore allegiance. In order to prevent the League from becoming a State within the State like the Protestant confederations, Henri III demonstrated great Catholic zeal and became the head of this association. He recommended it to governors and began to secretly prepare his revenge against the Huguenots. Yet the king was heavily indebted to his creditors and his poorly paid troops made up for their losses through pillage. The king was forced to unite the Estates General at Blois in 1576 to convince them of sacrifices they needed to make and to seek approval for war. The privileged orders, clergy and nobles, endorsed his war intentions but the third order expressed a desire for peace. As for finances, all three orders initially refused additional subsidies for the king, and in the

42. Miquel, *Guerres de religion*, 315–16.

43. Miquel, *Guerres de religion*, 318–20.

44. Miquel, *Guerres de religion*, 321–22.

end only the clergy relented and provided financial support. After further deliberations, and at the news of conquests and massacres at the hands of the Huguenots, the decision was made to suppress Reformed worship and to banish pastors and deacons. The Edict of Beaulieu was revoked by the assembly and armed conflict resumed, commencing the sixth war of religion. Although the king was beset with financial difficulties, he could not back away from a war he started. The Huguenots lost several cities including La Rochelle and negotiations led to the Peace of Bergerac in September 1577. This treaty was later confirmed by the Edict of Poitiers, signed the following month in October 1577 which followed the main points of the Edict of Beaulieu although with some new restrictions. Protestants were no longer in a position of strength to negotiate more favorable terms. Reformed worship was limited in many places, the zone of exclusion around Paris was enlarged, yet the Huguenots were guaranteed several more years of security for eight strongholds.[45]

The continued presence of the League after the Edict of Poitiers presented more disadvantages than advantages for Henri III. Public opinion failed to understand how a king could become leader of a political or religious faction. The king feared the Duke of Guise who used the League to further his own schemes, forming a political party, finding resources, and gathering men to his cause. The League clearly held an Ultramontane position which advocated the superiority of the pope over sovereigns, and favored closer relations with Rome, as did the house of Guise. The queen mother warned her son of the dangers and the king realized the error he made in becoming the head of the League. Putting an end to the League might have led to the end of the Wars of Religion had it not been for princely rivalry among Navarre, Condé, the Duke of Anjou, the Duke of Mayenne, and the young François de Chatillon, son of Coligny. In the quest to advance their own interests, a seventh war loomed on the horizon.[46]

SEVENTH WAR OF RELIGION (1579–1580)

The Edict of Poitiers was not widely received and in many places was not executed. There was division among the royal family and anarchy throughout the kingdom. How would order be restored in the kingdom? Once again Catherine de Médicis hitched her carriage and embarked on

45. Stéphan, *L'Épopée huguenote*, 149–51.
46. Miquel, *Guerres de religion*, 326–28.

a journey in 1578 to hold audiences with political leaders. She met Henri de Navarre who gathered leaders from churches throughout Languedoc. The negotiations resulted in the Treaty of Nérac on February 28, 1579, to provide clarification for the terms of peace. Catherine consented to respect the security of fourteen strongholds for six months, but she refused to grant freedom of worship. She settled for these short-lived treaties which satisfied her vanity and gave her the role of mediator.[47]

The seventh war which followed the Treaty of Nérac was on a smaller scale than previous ones and became known as the war of princes. In November 1579, Henri de Condé, who was not part of the negotiations at Nérac, seized La Fère. Although he was governor of the region, the Catholic population had not submitted to this authority. Catherine requested to see the prince and proposed a marriage to make Condé the brother-in-law of the king. Condé refused and La Fère was later retaken. He was chased from the city and escaped to Germany. There were disturbances in Dauphiné and Provence which were ransacked by looters. In May 1580, Henri de Navarre, leader of the Protestant party since 1576, seized the city of Cahors after a three-day battle. The prestige of his victory was so great that the Protestants of the Midi declared him the protector of their churches.[48] Lacking support from local Huguenots and leaders, the royal troops regained control of the city and Henri de Navarre was imprisoned in Cahors. Several skirmishes took place before the signing of the Treaty of Fleix in November 1580, which merely confirmed the Edict of Poitiers. The Protestants were promised six years to retain their strongholds without royal interference. To many people the seventh war seemed unnecessary and motivated by personal interests and rivalries.[49]

EIGHTH WAR OF RELIGION (1585-1598)

This eighth war of religion is often presented as the war of the three Henris—Henri III, Henri de Guise, and Henri de Navarre, with this latter Henri eventually victorious. With the death in 1584 of François d'Alençon, Duke of Anjou, and the last brother of King Henri III, Henri de Navarre became a legitimate heir to the throne.[50] The prospect of a Protestant king led to

47. Stéphan, *L'Épopée huguenote*, 151.
48. Miquel, *Guerres de religion*, 329–30.
49. Stéphan, *L'Épopée huguenote*, 152.
50. Miquel, *Guerres de religion*, 330.

the formation of another Catholic League led by Henri de Guise who was accompanied by his two brothers, Charles de Lorraine, Duke of Mayenne (1554–1611) and Louis, cardinal and archbishop of Reims. In March 1585, Henri III initiated an offensive to defend the Roman Catholic religion from heresy. Cardinal Charles de Bourbon, uncle of Henri de Navarre, and the brother of Antoine and Louis I, prince of Condé, was declared the sole candidate under the name of Charles X. Behind this designation were the three sons of François de Guise. The eldest, Henri de Guise, dreamed of the crown for himself and fancied himself a descendant of Charlemagne. This announcement triggered the eighth war of religion.[51]

As the League established control over northern France, cities resisted in southern France, such as Bordeaux and Marseilles. Henri III, then isolated in Paris, was forced by Henri de Guise to sign the Treaty of Nemours on July 7, 1585. The edict which followed renounced all previous edicts of pacification and forbade Calvinist worship. In 1576 Henri III had sought to exploit religious passions for his own interests. Now the League imposed on the king its leaders, its program, and its soldiers. If the Edict of Saint-Maur had been painful, the Edict of Nemours was more traumatic. Both freedom of worship and freedom of conscience were restricted. Huguenots had to choose between recanting or exile within six months. Pastors were banished and stronghold cities were to be surrendered. Neighbors and village priests were recruited and paid by the State to spy on and denounce recalcitrant Protestants. There were massive abjurations and confiscation of possessions.[52] Henri III tried in vain to convince his cousin and brother-in-law Henri de Navarre to convert to Catholicism. His efforts were cut short when Henri de Navarre was excommunicated by the papal bull of Pope Sixtus V in 1585, deemed extreme even by moderate Catholics and Parliament. Henri de Navarre and the prince of Condé had recently renewed their alliance with Damville and sought support from England and the Protestant princes of Denmark and Germany. Navarre proclaimed that their armies were not opposed to the king, but to the tyranny of the Guises. Catherine, as always, hoped to convince Navarre to abjure. The Guises besieged Sedan and Hametz which threatened Lorraine. Royal military operations under Duke Anne de Joyeuse in the southwest led to acts of violence, and the executions of prisoners were glorified by Catholic preachers. Then, at the Battle of Coutras on October 20, 1587, the first major battle for the king

51. Stéphan, *L'Épopée huguenote*, 153.
52. Foa, "Les droits fragiles," 103–4.

of Navarre, the royal army led by Joyeuse was defeated and the duke killed in battle. Henri IV returned the body to the family and attended a Mass in honor of the deceased enemies.[53]

On February 8, 1587, Mary Stuart, Queen of France and of Scots, a cousin of the Guises, was executed for treason. She had been raised in France and married the French dauphin who later became King François II. After her husband's death she returned to Scotland to assume her role as the country's monarch. Her death led to the accusation that Henri III was the accomplice of Elizabeth of England under whose reign Catholics suffered. In Paris, the League made the law and there was talk of deposing the king. They sought a return to the Middle Ages with limited royal power, a powerful clergy, and an independent nobility. The project of Philip II to invade England emboldened the fanatics who believed that heresy was on the verge of being crushed. Victories on the battlefield had increased the prestige of the Duke of Guise, now called the pillar of the Church. When the agitation grew in Paris, Henri III forbade Henri de Guise to return there. The duke hastened to reach Paris and at his arrival in the city he was wildly acclaimed by the crowds. Henri III recalled his troops to defend the city and panic-stricken Parisians rose up to defend the city in an event known as the Day of the Barricades (*la journée des barricades*) on May 12, 1588. The royal troops were halted by the crowds, the Swiss guards were massacred, and members of the League took control of the city. Henri III, humiliated, took refuge in Chartres and signed the Edict of Union on July 15, 1588 which confirmed the Treaty of Nemours. The king promised to banish heresy and rejected as his successor any heretical prince. He granted amnesty for those involved in the events at Paris and confirmed the elections made by the League. Henri de Guise was appointed lieutenant general of the royal army and important positions were attributed to his accomplices. The most extreme Catholics had triumphed.[54]

In October 1588, in front of the representatives of the three orders (*trois états*)[55] dominated by the members of the League, Henri III again solemnly swore an oath to abolish heresy. He was acclaimed by the deputies and together they sang the *Te Deum* at Saint-Sauveur. At the same time, the king warned the members of the League that they endangered Catholicism

53. Stéphan, *L'Épopée huguenote*, 154–56.

54. Stéphan, *L'Épopée huguenote*, 157; Miquel, *Guerres de religion*, 348.

55. French society was composed of three orders (*les trois états*): clergy, nobility, and peasantry (*le tiers-état*).

through their factiousness. Later, after he had overhauled his government, the king decided to destroy the League which he considered dangerous for the monarchy and for peace. Henri III dreamed of eliminating his archenemy the Duke of Guise who flattered himself in boasting that he held the king prisoner. The king resolved to follow the counsel of his entourage who repeatedly advised the king that it was not possible to rid himself of his antagonist by normal means of justice. Two months later, on December 23, in the Castle of Blois, Henri de Guise, having been summoned by the king, was stabbed to death by the king's guards. Others associated with the house of Guise were arrested, including the archbishop of Lyon, the old cardinal of Bourbon, and the cardinal of Guise, the latter executed the following day. The bodies of the duke and cardinal were burned and tossed into the Loire River. News of Henri de Guise's death spread rapidly. Paris took up arms and the Sorbonne proclaimed the king deposed. Outward signs of the monarchy were destroyed and images of the king lacerated. There were collective prayers of purification, and penitent processions united the people to restore religious unity and to remove the stain of heresy. For many, Henri III was no longer the king of France and was declared a tyrant. The Sorbonne freed the people from their oath of fidelity to the Crown. Parliament members who had remained faithful to the king were insulted and the most ardent royalists arrested. The League named the Duke of Mayenne as lieutenant general of the armies to replace the Duke of Guise. An ideological shift took place with the claim that one becomes king by popular consent.[56]

Henri III left Blois and took shelter in Tours where the Parliament was transferred. The Duke of Mayenne headed to Tours with his horsemen and scattered the royal forces at Amboise. Many provinces were in the hands of League members. Henri III, chased from Paris, had no other choice than to seek reconciliation with Henri de Navarre for a common front against Mayenne. Navarre's vanguard stopped Mayenne's forces at the outskirts of Tours. Mayenne's army was beaten by François de Châtillon near Chartres and Navarre convinced Henri III to march on Paris. Their combined armies marched toward Paris with forty thousand troops and camped near Pontoise in preparation for the assault.[57]

At Paris, the population railed against their sovereign for having formed an alliance with the heretics. On August 1, 1589, Jacques Clément, a Dominican monk belonging to the League, decided to take action after

56. Stéphan, *L'Épopée huguenote*, 158–59; Miquel, *Guerres de religion*, 349–51.

57. Stéphan, *L'Épopée huguenote*, 159; Miquel, *Guerres de religion*, 352–53.

consultation with a theologian. With a letter of recommendation from Achille de Harlay, president of the Paris parliament, he was able to obtain a meeting with Henri III at Saint-Cloud. The monk requested permission to deliver a private message to the king. Alone with the king, Clément stabbed Henri III in the stomach as he leaned in to better hear the message. The assassin was immediately killed by the king's guards. That evening, shortly before his death, joined by Henri de Navarre and attended by physicians, the king enjoined Henri de Navarre to convert to Catholicism and recognized him as his successor. It was reported that Henri III died making the sign of the cross. Since the beginning of the wars many grand seigneurs had been assassinated. This was the first regicide![58]

Henri de Navarre was the heir presumptive to the throne of France at the age of thirty-five, a king without a kingdom. France needed a king capable of standing up to Philip II of Spain. Catholics knew that Navarre disapproved of the murder of the two members of the house of Guise. They also recognized him as a valiant prince from his exploits in battle. Moderate Catholics held in common with Navarre the hatred of the pope, fear of the Spanish, and disdain for the Guises. In the spirit of Gallicanism, they were committed to the independence of the Church from Rome, and they were ready to welcome a king who could reestablish peace and guarantee the coexistence of two religions. They were prepared to oppose the League in order to establish a monarchy no longer at the mercy of religion. Yet to be king, Navarre needed to be chosen not simply crowned. There was opposition from the League and many nobles who would not recognize him as Henri III's successor. Once again the king was invited to convert and refused.[59]

On August 4, 1589, Henri de Navarre rendered a public declaration designed to appease the factions but which in reality fully satisfied no one. He promised that the Catholic religion would maintain its place of preeminence and that he would seek instruction in this religion through a council within six months. During this time, Catholics and Protestants would keep their respective places and Reformed worship was limited to the places where it was already observed. Based on this promise, there were many who rallied to his cause, who desired a return to order and the cessation of violence. Among them were two royal princes, Conti and Montpensier, Catholics, and parliamentarians. Others conditioned the acceptance of the

58. Stéphan, L'Épopée huguenote, 159–60; Miquel, Guerres de religion, 353–54.

59. Miquel, Guerres de religion, 355–59.

king on his conversion to Catholicism. Protestants hesitated, concerned that Navarre had left open the door for his conversion.[60]

During the years 1588 and 1589 Henri de Navarre multiplied military activity in Normandy and around Paris. His royal troops, composed of Protestants and Catholics, defeated the Duke of Mayenne at Arques near Dieppe in September 1589 and besieged a resistant Paris. In March 1590, the famous battle of Ivry near Dreux opened the way for a new siege of Paris with its fifty thousand–strong militias who once again preferred famine to heresy. A complete blockade of the city worsened living conditions and led to widespread famine and illness. Only the intervention of Spanish troops forced the lifting of the siege in September. A few months later there was a failed attempt to enter the city with soldiers disguised as merchants.[61] A climate of terror enveloped the city with executions which included Barnabe Brisson (1531–1591), the president of Parliament, hanged from a beam in council chambers. The excesses ended with the arrival of Charles of Mayenne who eliminated the fanatics who had petitioned Philip II to provide a king and had sown terror in the city.[62] During this period, Charles X, king of the League and prisoner of the royals, died. Navarre continued to battle in Normandy, failed to take Rouen and Orléans, and suffered several defeats at the hand of Mayenne assisted by Spanish troops. Since January 1592, Mayenne had begun negotiations with Philip II in the event Philip sought to obtain the throne for his daughter Isabella through marriage. Mayenne had also sent Villeroy to negotiate with supporters of Navarre with no success. Mayenne demanded beforehand the conversion of Henri de Navarre and even made a declaration to rally Catholic lords to his candidacy. Navarre demanded recognition as king before his conversion. Catholic priests in Paris swore to die before accepting Navarre as king, even if he converted. In the end, Navarre understood that as a Huguenot he would never be accepted by the Catholics. In order for hostilities to cease. Navarre confirmed his intention to convert to the Catholic religion.[63]

For over thirty years during the Wars of Religion, the Huguenots survived during times of prohibition and temporary legality. The alternance of periods of gain and loss perhaps did more than anything else to traumatize the Protestant minority. Before the wars, their repression and martyrdom

60. Miquel, *Guerres de religion*, 361.
61. Miquel, *Guerres de religion*, 374.
62. Miquel, *Guerres de religion*, 380–81.
63. Miquel, *Guerres de religion*, 383–86.

had increased their numbers. Their legalization led them to establish themselves, buy houses, start businesses, with false hope and a sense of security that was ripped from them according to the monarch's caprices. They were often left with the choice of conversion or exile. The loss of rights they had obtained did more to shatter the Protestant momentum than the absence of rights.[64] It is estimated that from 1570 to 1598 Protestants lost 30 percent of their places of worship. They found themselves on the outside of a Catholic and royal consensus. For half a century Reformed believers were hunted, massacred, exiled from their cities, chased from their offices and places of employment, deprived of basic rights, and wearied by financial sacrifice.[65] There were further struggles as Henri IV worked to rid the kingdom of Spain's influence. The clemency of the king toward those who had viciously resisted him won over much of the opposition. The crowning moment of Henri IV's reign would arrive with the Edict of Nantes in 1598.

64. Foa, "Les droits fragiles," 107.

65. Garrisson, *Histoire des protestants*, 67–70.

Chapter 6

The Edict of Nantes

IN THE LAST CHAPTER we saw that Henri de Navarre became the titular head of France in 1589 after the assassination of Henri III, whose marriage to Louise de Lorraine produced no heir. Another legitimate heir, Henri III's brother François, Duke of Anjou, had died prematurely in 1584. Under Salic Law, the next heir was Henri de Navarre, married to Marguerite de Valois, daughter of Henri II and Catherine de Médicis. After years of attempts to deny the throne to Navarre, his enemies realized they could not defeat him militarily. He adopted the religion of the majority of his subjects in order to assure the freedom of conscience to those with whom he shared a faith and who had fought by his side. This decision appeared to proceed from an honorable and legitimate concern for the peace and unity of the nation. There were concessions including his declaration on August 4, 1589 that Catholicism would remain the religion of the kingdom. Although the royal princes, officers, and nobles of the court swore allegiance to him, the Catholic League, supported by Philip II, recognized the cardinal of Bourbon, under the name Charles X, as the legitimate king. This action had sparked the last of the eight sixteenth-century Wars of Religion.[1]

Modern historians have generally lauded Henri IV for having sacrificed his religious scruples of conscience and adopting the religion of the majority of French people in the best interests of the nation to end the interminable civil wars. There are exceptions among Protestant historians who have questioned the necessity of the king's conversion to Catholicism. In any case, Henri IV had measured the strength of the Catholic Church in

1. Stéphan, *L'Épopée huguenote*, 163.

France. Although he had great military successes early on, the failed siege at Paris had broken his élan. Henri IV struggled to take back his kingdom from the influence of Philip II of Spain. After three years of conflict the Treaty or Peace of Vervins was signed with the intervention of the pope who worried about the ruin of Catholic powers. The clauses of the earlier 1559 Treaty of Cateau-Cambrésis, which had marked the end of the struggle between Spain and France for the control of Italy, were reestablished. The treaty also signaled the end of Spanish dominance. Philip II was near death and had not succeeded in taking a single province or city from France. The English were the masters of the seas and the Dutch had constituted an independent state grouping seven maritime provinces. Perhaps it was this reality of powerlessness which resolved Henri IV to sacrifice his religion in spite of his reluctance. After decades of war, France was exhausted. The population had been decimated, the countryside devastated, roads crumbled, bridges collapsed, cities razed, villages destroyed, and the nation deeply in debt. The nation was in a desperate condition and there seemed no end to the struggles. Yet the kingdom, by its resistance to foreign powers, had proven its vitality. Slowly the kingdom would dress its wounds and come back to life.[2] The Edict of Nantes was a watershed in French history. France sought to establish the notion of tolerance and officially proclaimed for the first time that people are free to profess the religion of their choice. Yet this innovation should be seen more as the work of circumstances rather than volition. The arrival of a Protestant king and the weariness of opposing parties imposed this compromise, one which would not last. One law, one king, one faith remained the dominating principle. It was only a question of how long the regime of Henri IV would survive.[3]

The Edict of Nantes was preceded by Henri IV's conversion from Protestantism to Catholicism. His closest friends, Duplessis-Mornay and Agrippa d'Aubigné, implored him to remain faithful to his religion. The archbishop of Bourges announced Henri's intention to return to Catholicism on May 17, 1593. Two months later, on July 25, 1593, Henri IV solemnly recanted in the Basilica of Saint-Denis at the feet of the archbishop.[4] His abjuration was attacked as feigned by some preachers in Paris, yet many citizens simply wanted peace, order, a king, and a united nation free from foreign influence. Protestants did not hide their chagrin and an assembly

2. Stéphan, *L'Épopée huguenote*, 169–72; Miquel, *Guerres de religion*, 395.

3. Stéphan, *L'Épopée huguenote*, 173–74.

4. Stéphan, *L'Épopée huguenote*, 168–69.

gathered at Mantes for several months from October 1593 until January 1594. They requested guarantees from the king who promised to rees-tablish the edict of 1577 and its guarantee of religious tolerance, as well as the Treaty of Fleix from 1580. Huguenots were permitted to worship throughout the kingdom, even discreetly at the court, and army officials could celebrate the Lord's Supper in the camps. With these conditions, the Protestants provisionally maintained their confidence in Henri IV.[5]

Gradually the leaders of the League rallied to Henri IV which led to his coronation as King Henri IV at the Cathedral of Chartres on February 27, 1594. There he pronounced the traditional oath to drive out from his lands all heretics denounced by the Church. On March 22, the king entered Paris and the *Te Deum* rang out from Notre Dame. Pope Clement VIII, vexed by the French Church's absolution of Henri IV without pontifical authorization, distrusted the sincerity of the king. Not until September 1595 did the pope grant his conditional pardon. The Huguenots, however, ulcerated by the king's abjuration, feared that reconciliation with the pope would lead to renewed persecution, and sought to obtain guarantees of security. The king had demanded Catholic leaders to cease persecution in violation of the terms of the Edict of Mantes, which in 1591 revoked the most rigorous of Henri III's edicts against the Huguenots. Henri IV had even tacitly authorized Reformed worship with discretion in royal cities. Still, the favor he showed towards Catholics worried his former friends. After the end of the civil wars, there were still excesses of passion and in-tolerance. In 1595 two hundred Huguenots worshipping at Châtaigneraie in Vendée were massacred. In response to the continuing violence, the king promulgated an edict of pacification, declared as perpetual and irrevocable, the Edict of Nantes on April 13, 1598. The edict, which imposed religious coexistence, was met with resistance. Rome continued to resist any change in the Catholic Church's privileged position in France. Pope Clement VIII declared that freedom of conscience was the worst thing to ever happen in the world. Henri IV deployed his energy to obtain the registering of the edict in regional parliaments. The Parliament of Rouen did not register the edict until 1609.[6] After years of religious wars, the edict did not im-mediately extinguish all the grudges and resentment. But it opened a new period in relations between Catholics and Protestants and provided relative security and tolerance for the Huguenots. The Peace of Vervins, signed on

5. Miquel, *Guerres de religion*, 388.

6. Stéphan, *L'Épopée huguenote*, 172–73; Miquel, *Guerres de religion*, 389.

May 5, 1598, between Henri IV and Philip II of Spain, brought a temporary entente between the two nations and contributed to Henri IV's rising stature in the affirmation of his power and the stability of his reign. The birth of Louis XIII in 1601 assured the perennity of the dynasty.[7]

PROVISIONS OF THE EDICT OF NANTES

The Edict of Nantes was Henri IV's crowning achievement. The document has four distinct texts. The first text consists of ninety-two general articles declared "permanent and irrevocable." The second text with fifty-six articles granted exemptions from the general articles and application in specific situations. The last two documents were called *brevets* and were provisional in nature. This was an edict of compromise previously unknown in France which granted legal recognition of the Protestant religion and set limits to Protestant worship. Under the terms of the edict, Protestants were granted substantial religious rights and a measure of religious liberty. In other words, freedom of conscience and conditional freedom of worship.[8] Protestants were still required to pay tithes to Catholic parish priests, observe Catholic feast days, and all religious property that had originally belonged to the Catholic Church was ordered returned. From a religious point of view, the edict granted considerable concessions to the Protestants, notably in the institution of the principle of freedom of conscience in all the kingdom, freedom to change one's religion, and freedom of worship in all the regions where Protestantism was established before 1597, in cities and towns, and in the chateaux of nobles with a maximum of thirty persons. In other places, in and around Paris, Protestant worship was forbidden within an established radius. Protestants and Catholics had equal rights in providing education for their children. From a political point of view, full amnesty was granted for all acts of war. Civil equality with Catholics was guaranteed and there was a provision for the right of access to public employment. Those who had fled France were allowed to return.[9]

The edict opened access for Protestants to universities and public offices, and four academies were granted authorization along with the right to convoke religious synods. Protestants were guaranteed the security of their garrisons for eight years in several towns, most notably the port city

---

7. Giraudier, "La rébellion du duc de Bouillon," 339.

8. Daireaux, "Louis XIV et les protestants normands," 124.

9. Stéphan, *L'Épopée huguenote*, 173.

of La Rochelle. One great novelty was that civil power placed limits on religious domination of society. In the preceding centuries, the Catholic princes of Europe told their subjects to believe what they believed. Dissenters were treated as heretics for the crimes of sacrilege and blasphemy. Most often, these princes were merely the docile executioners of an intolerant Church. Unsurprisingly, the edict was not accepted without the protest of the Church although there were provisions for the Church's benefit. The Catholic Church recuperated two hundred cities and two thousand rural parishes. Finally, the Church resigned herself to tolerance as a necessity of the circumstances of the time. When the Church no longer had the princes in her hand to destroy false religion and pursue heretics, she practiced patience until the tide turned again in her favor. While Protestants were not allowed missionary activity to open new places of worship, Catholics were able to alter the religious map in opening churches in places where Catholicism had disappeared.[10] In reality the Edict of Nantes was a treaty with concessions designed to prevent further warfare. The edict, in granting tolerance toward Protestants, had actually prescribed the reestablishment of the rights of the Catholic Church. Article 3 stipulated that the Catholic, Apostolic, and Roman religion would be reestablished throughout the kingdom to be freely and peacefully exercised without any trouble or obstacle. Henri IV had pronounced the return to the pre-war status quo as presented in the late 1550s. This authorized the full and complete institutional restoration of the Catholic Church in every corner of the kingdom even in places where the majority of habitants had converted to the Reformed faith, in cities like La Rochelle, Montauban, and Montpellier, and in vast regions like the Cévennes, Dauphiné, and Vivarais. In all these places, Protestants now needed to prepare for the return of priests where they had not been seen for two generations.[11] In cities where Protestantism had won the day there had been no Catholic presence for forty years. The reestablishment of Catholic worship in these places seemed strange, even absurd. Catholic processions resumed in places where there had been none for decades. From a Catholic presence to a Catholic reconquest was only a step. Tensions were often high in cities with two places of worship, two cemeteries, two categories of the king's subjects, and even two church bells.[12]

10. Miquel, *Guerres de religion*, 407.

11. Birnstiel, "La conversion des protestants," 95–96.

12. Miquel, *Guerres de religion*, 409.

The edict's importance lay in a changed perspective of the individual. As political subject, the individual was expected to obey the king, regardless of confession. As a believer, the subject was free to choose his religion which was now considered a private matter. Protestants retained territorial possession of places of safety in more than one hundred cities in France, including La Rochelle, Saumur, Montpellier and Montauban. During this period of tolerance, these cities became states within the State. They held political assemblies, developed territorial organization, maintained military fortresses, and practiced diplomacy and relations with foreign powers, notably England. La Rochelle became the principal bastion of the Reformed religion and was supported by England which sought to curb the development and expansion of the French navy.[13]

The civil peace established by the king was not met with religious peace. Inside the competing parties, seemingly reconciled to the king, there was not unanimity on the guarantees offered by the edict. Protestants were divided in their level of confidence in the king's ability to enforce the edict's clauses. There were two major tendencies among Protestants and the division of Protestants was seen as a sign of weakness which the young Louis XIII (1601–1643) and his mother would later exploit.[14] Those who followed Duplessis-Mornay (1549–1623), faithful companion of Henri IV in his political and military struggles, thought the edict would guarantee long years of peace. Others disagreed and aligned with Henri de Rohan (1579–1638), who considered it prudent for churches to remain mobilized with the likelihood of future wars. The former supposed that there was nothing to fear from the Counter-Reformation which had undertaken the reconquest of souls throughout Europe. Perhaps they even hoped, along with Henri IV, for a reconciliation of the Christian family in the framework of a national Church, independent from Rome. In truth, the Edict of Nantes provided more satisfaction to the Huguenot party, to the nobility, and to cities than to the religion itself which was merely tolerated. The king was faithful to his oath at Saint-Denis and remained Catholic.[15]

13. Carenco, L'Édit de Nantes, 3.

14. Garrisson, Histoire des protestants, 126.

15. Miquel, Guerres de religion, 399–400.

DISMANTLING THE EDICT OF NANTES

The king honored his promises and the edict was enforced during the reign of Henri IV, at times with great difficulty, until his assassination in 1610. He survived multiple plots and attempts to assassinate him before falling at the hand of a Catholic zealot, François Ravaillac, on May 14, 1610. His death alarmed the Protestants who feared the loss of their acquired rights. Marie de Médicis (1575–1642) became queen following her husband's death. She confirmed the Edict of Nantes in a declaration May 22, 1610, but Protestants had little confidence in her. She was described as easily influenced and dominated by her sister Léonora Galigal and her husband Concino Concini (1569–1617). The Estates General gathered in 1614 and 1615 at which the Protestants perceived that the nobility and the clergy were prepared to consider the edicts of pacification as provisory. They were also alarmed by the proposed marriage of Louis XIII to Anne d'Autriche. Three provinces, Languedoc, Guyenne, and Poitou took part in an uprising led by malcontent lords. Marie's negotiations with them resulted in the Treaty of Loudun which granted six more years of protection for Protestant cities of safety. Shortly after, Louis XIII, anxious to rid himself of his mother's yoke, had Concini assassinated on April 24, 1617. His mother withdrew to Blois and attempted to foment a conspiracy against her son which failed.[16]

The protections enjoyed under Henri IV began to unravel and were gradually removed after his death. Long before its revocation, the edict was undermined through tortured interpretations, by inconsistent application, and interminable bad faith complaints lodged against the Huguenots. The Huguenots were accused of trying to establish a State within the State as the pontifical power had already done. The Edict of Nantes had not established equality between the religions. Protestants received political advantages and remained religiously disadvantaged.[17] The Huguenots were simply tolerated as long as they practiced their religion within the strictures imposed on them. Following the Edict of Nantes, the first ten years of the seventeenth century marked a Catholic renewal. New congregations appeared and convents were established. Even the king flattered himself that France would return to religious unity. To this end funds were established (*caisse de conversion*) to pay pastors who converted to Catholicism. Henri IV also applied an edict to the Huguenots, amended by Catholic clergy, to

16. Stéphan, *L'Épopée huguenote*, 206–8.

17. Garrisson, *Histoire des protestants*, 124.

allow the fortifications of secure cities to fall into ruin in reducing the funds previously promised for their maintenance. Political Huguenot assemblies which gathered every three years protested in vain against the abuses and vexations.[18] Unquestionably the times had changed from religious wars to religious controversies and were marked by conversions between the two religions; monks embraced the Reformed religion and pastors turned toward Catholicism. Henri IV had several Protestant collaborators and to his credit during the fifteen years of his reign he lifted his worn nation out of over thirty years of civil war. Among his faults was his refusal to reunite the Estates General and to create a parliamentary monarchy which might have protected the nation from coming abuses of power. He oriented the nation toward an absolutism which offered him a stunning if brief splendor which would lead to bloody reactions. Another serious fault was in recalling the Jesuits from exile which resulted in their monopoly of the educational system.[19]

The presence of Protestant strongholds became intolerable for Henri IV's successor, his son Louis XIII. Under him the domination of the Catholic clergy grew rapidly. The king took a Jesuit for confessor and his new minister, Charles-Albert de Luynes, pledged to exterminate the heretics. At the general assembly of Catholic clergy in 1617, Louis XIII, instead of respecting the will of his father, ordered the restitution of possessions to the Catholic Church. At this time, three-quarters of Navarre and Béarn were Huguenots but their leaders were unable to persuade the king to reverse his decision. Once the king reconciled with his mother, he marched on the province of Béarn, took the stronghold of Navarriens, and reestablished Catholicism. The abuses committed against a majority Calvinist population foreshadowed the future *dragonnades*.[20] In response to the king's actions, the Huguenot general assembly at La Rochelle in December 1620 divided France into eight quasi-military regions with leaders which triggered Catholic opposition. Most of the Midi took up arms but the rest of the country did not move against the king. He went on to besiege Montauban which resisted heroically for two and a half months and forced the king to lift the siege November 2, 1621. At Paris, the wrath of the fanatics erupted,

18. Stéphan, *L'Épopée huguenote*, 202–3.

19. Stéphan, *L'Épopée huguenote*, 204–5.

20. *Dragonnades* were a form of persecution under Louis XIV. Protestants were forced to lodge the king's cavalrymen (*dragons*) to induce Protestants to convert to Catholicism (*Nouveau Petit Robert*, 783).

especially upon hearing about the death of Mayenne at Montauban. The populace massacred Huguenots returning from their temple at Charenton and burned the edifice. There were other failed attempts of resistance by Huguenot leaders leading to further massacres with an unforgettable cruelty at Négrepelisse and Saint-Antonin, the royal forces led by Condé, recent convert to Catholicism. Great Huguenot lords surrendered and were recompensed with titles and positions. Rohan was the exception. The king besieged Montpellier in August 1622 but the city defended itself so valiantly that the king agreed to negotiate. The siege was lifted and the Peace of Montpellier, signed on October 18, 1622, confirmed the Edict of Nantes and granted amnesty, but forbade political assemblies without royal authorization. Also, only two stronghold cities remained, La Rochelle and Montauban.[21] The years 1622 to 1625 were marked by incessant squabbles and acts of violence between the parties. In 1625, Rohan in Languedoc and his brother Soubise in the West engaged in military campaigns without decisive results. Cardinal Richelieu's attempts to negotiate with La Rochelle failed in 1625, and the Peace of Paris, signed on February 5, 1626, maintained the status quo until Richelieu was in a position of strength to subdue the rebels.[22]

CARDINAL RICHELIEU AND THE SIEGE OF LA ROCHELLE

Marie de Médicis had succeeded in introducing Armand du Plessis de Richelieu (1585–1642), now wearing a cardinal's hat, into the court of Louis XIII in 1624. Richelieu held the position of prime minister during the reign of Louis XIII (r. 1610–1643). He was a man of great ambition and capacities, a strict defender of the Catholic cause in France with the intention to break all opposition to royal absolutism. He would battle the Huguenots more out of political than religious motives.[23] Louis XIII and Richelieu sought to force the submission of Protestants to royal authority and reinforce the unity of the kingdom. The city of La Rochelle stood as a formidable barrier to their designs and had become the principal stronghold of the Huguenot party. La Rochelle had largely adhered to the Protestant Reformation, was responsible for the dissemination of Protestantism

21. Stéphan, L'Épopée huguenote, 208–11; Miquel, Guerres de religion, 425–26.

22. Garrisson, Histoire des protestants, 127.

23. Delumeau, Le christianisme, 97.

in western regions of France, and had become a refuge for Protestants fleeing other places. Richelieu had been forced to sign the Treaty of Paris in February 1626, was criticized by the Ultramontanes, and the compromise became a personal embarrassment. Richelieu confessed that as long as the Huguenots existed in France, the king would never be complete master of the kingdom nor would he ever be able to undertake any glorious actions outside the kingdom. He would not pardon the Huguenots for their audacity and created a French naval force capable of blockading La Rochelle without depending on foreign powers.[24] In 1627 the conflict was reignited and La Rochelle was besieged for a year, encircled and cut off from all outside provision. Richelieu ordered the construction of an enormous dike to prevent all help from the sea. The last months of the siege were marked by a devastating famine, obliging women, children, and the elderly to leave the city and wander destitute through the marshes where few survived. Those besieged survived by eating horses, dogs and cats, with hundreds dying daily of famine. La Rochelle had a population of twenty-five thousand before the siege, of which eighteen thousand were Protestant, and little more than five thousand when the blockade ended. The expedition mounted by the Duke of Buckingham failed due to his assassination and La Rochelle capitulated October 28, 1628. The next day Richelieu entered the city and celebrated a solemn mass in the Church of Sainte-Marguerite. Louis XIII entered La Rochelle on November 1 to receive its surrender followed by a great procession on November 3. The king abolished all the former benefits the city enjoyed, ordered most of the ramparts leveled, turned the churches over to the Catholic Church, and created a bishopric. The fall of La Rochelle was celebrated throughout the kingdom, and Pope Urban VIII (1568–1644) addressed his felicitations to the *roi très chrétien*. Louis XIII had the Notre-Dame des Victoires built at Paris in honor of his triumph. Ten years later he would consecrate France to the Holy Virgin and institute the Feast of the Assumption. After years of sacrifice, La Rochelle's destiny was now tied to the French monarchy and the Catholic Church. Together they had sought to subdue the souls of this rebellious Protestant stronghold which resisted Paris and Rome for sixty years, and finally emerged victorious.[25]

After the fall of La Rochelle, Rohan renewed the act of union between the Huguenots in January 1629 and the decision was made to continue the war. Rohan continued the resistance, appealed to the Swiss and even the

24. Stéphan, *L'Épopée huguenote*, 211–13.
25. Stéphan, *L'Épopée huguenote*, 214–15.

Spanish for military assistance. Louis XIII, at the head of the royal army, defeated Charles Emmanuel at the Suza Pass, signed a treaty with the English, and turned his attention against the Huguenots with the siege of Privas. The city fell and suffered severe reprisals. Royal troops then marched through the Cévennes, Alès capitulated and the regions of Montauban, Castres, and Millau were ravaged. In June 1629 with the Edict of Grace or Peace of Alès under Louis XIII, negotiated by Richelieu with Huguenot leaders, the Huguenots experienced the loss of many earlier gains and churches were in the hands of the king with only his word as a guarantee to respect the edicts. The edict maintained the concessions of the Edict of Nantes but dismantled the Protestant party. Reformed pastors had the right to preach, celebrate the Lord's Supper, baptize, and officiate at marriages only in villages and cities authorized by the Edict of Nantes. Protestants, who had contributed to the restoration of the unity of the kingdom were now considered factious in the face of a centralized unity sought by the great ministers, Richelieu and later Mazarin. What would become of the estimated 865,000 Protestants, of entire regions where Protestants were in the majority, in Bas-Languedoc, the Cévennes, the south of Poitou? Their conversion was sought through threats and terror. The *dragonnades* replaced the Wars of Religion as Protestants lost their princes and protectors.[26] Louis XIII ordered the demolition of Protestant places of safety and the reestablishment of Catholic worship. Although the Huguenots theoretically retained religious rights for another fifty years, they lost political influence and were progressively excluded from public functions, These rights were slowly undermined under Louis XIII's successor, his son Louis XIV. The Edict of Nantes was maintained while awaiting the return of Protestants to the bosom of the Church. For Louis XIII, this was the Church in which all the kings which preceded him had lived without interruption or change for eleven hundred years. Henri de Rohan left France with his family and died on the battlefield at Rheinfeld in February 1638. As for Richelieu, after having defeated the political power of the Huguenots, he imagined that no longer having political influence, the Huguenot heresy would die out by itself with assistance from increased repression and conversions.[27] Huguenots died but the heresy did not. More extreme measures were needed. To them we now turn.

26. De Montclos, *Histoire religieuse*, 67; Miquel, *Guerres de religion*, 401–2.

27. Stéphan, *L'Épopée huguenote*, 216–17.

Chapter 7

The Edict of Revocation

Since the sixteenth century Protestants had struggled in their rapport with royal power. The proliferation of their petitions to kings testifies to their desire to place themselves under the protection of the king. At the same time, the realization that the monarch also held the authority to revoke what had been granted led to suspicion and mistrust toward rulers. The State held the authority to grant religious freedom without grounding these rights in anything but the power of the State or the word of the monarch. Protestants owed the recognition of their rights more to a sovereign decree than to an evolving society or anything approaching genuine tolerance or religious pluralism. These rights were incessantly challenged and undermined.[1] With the Revocation of the Edict of Nantes in 1685, by Louis XIV, grandson of Henri IV, Protestantism no longer had the right to exist in the kingdom, and the fiction that all the Protestants had been converted or exiled permitted the authorities to oblige the obstinate to attend mass.[2]

The Edict of Nantes under Henri IV had given Protestants protection and survived almost a century (1598–1685) before its revocation, during which time French Catholics and Protestants cohabitated in an uneasy peace with intermittent, regional conflicts, as in the siege of La Rochelle.[3] Paul Deschanel (1855–1922), deputy of Eure-et-Loir and future president of the Republic, called the Revocation of the Edict of Nantes, decided at Versailles in the shadows without discussion, one of the greatest crimes

1. Foa, "Les droits fragiles," 93.
2. Garrisson, *Histoire des protestants*, 185–86.
3. Dusseau, "L'histoire de la Séparation," 13.

ever committed against human conscience.[4] The Church and the monarchy remained collaborators in their intrigues as they plotted the suppression of heresy and the removal of protections provided under the Edict of Nantes.

LOUIS XIV AND CARDINAL MAZARIN

Louis XIII had declared his desire for the conversion of all those who belonged to the heretical religion and their return to the bosom of the Church. When he died on May 14, 1643, seven months after Richelieu, his son Louis XIV, grandson of Henri IV, was only five years old. The wife of Louis XIII, Anne d'Autriche became queen. As Marie de Médicis had accorded her favors to Richelieu, Anne acted in similar fashion toward Cardinal Mazarin (1602–1661) who became the master of the kingdom until his death. The Huguenots remained faithful to the Crown and a royal declaration in 1652 recognized their fidelity and promised the maintenance of the Edict of Nantes with the enjoyment of all its benefits. This promise from a fourteen-year old king would not last long. Mazarin himself has been described as a tolerant man who had granted employment and government positions to Huguenots. He had not given full satisfaction to the complaints of the clergy who protested the construction of temples and pathetically called on the king for protection as if the Catholic Church were in danger. Yet in 1656 he reversed the declaration of 1652 and forbade the exercise of Reformed religion in places where it had recently been established. In 1658, provincial synods sent a delegation to present their grievances to the king who received them after a four-month delay. The king granted them the authorization to hold a general synod in November 1659 at Loudun where the king's representative reproached the Huguenots for their insolence and announced that this would be their last general synod. An order was later given which required a Catholic royal commissioner at provincial synods.[5]

Early in Louis XIV's reign there was a season of religious tranquility for Protestants from 1643 to 1660. Perhaps a regime of reciprocal tolerance would have eventually succeeded if the most fanatical elements of the clergy had not continued their opposition. Louis XIV initially thought that the best way to reduce the number of Huguenots in his kingdom was to strictly respect what previous kings had done and refuse to grant them

4. Bruley, *La séparation*, 279.

5. Stéphan, *L'Épopée huguenote*, 221–24.

any additional rights.[6] Beginning in the 1660s the application of the Edict of Nantes was modified. Mazarin died on March 8, 1661 when Louis XIV was twenty-two years old and the king resolved to no longer tolerate any resistance to his orders. He claimed the divine right as God's representative on earth and was determined to become the absolute master of his kingdom which he ruled for another fifty-five years until 1715. It was left to Louis XIV to restrictively apply and then finally rescind the Edict of Nantes which reinaugurated decades of war, repression, and persecution. Protestants were once again denied the most basic religious and civil rights and excluded from most professions.[7]

A series of hostile measures was carried out to undermine the irrevocable edict of Louis XIV's great-grandfather, Henri IV. With the edict in hand, from 1660 to 1679 Louis XIV sought to paralyze Protestant vitality and bring about conversions to Catholicism. The king continued the practice of earlier kings with an institution known as *commissions* as the principal means of repression. The *commissions* under Henri III and Henri IV worked theoretically to reestablish the peace, find pragmatic solutions to facilitate the relations between Catholics and Protestants, and ensure coexistence between religions torn apart by hate and tenacious conflicts. New *commissions* were appointed in 1656 to judge infringements to the Edict of Nantes. Louis XIV appointed and sent commissioners in 1661 into the provinces to search out any violations of the Edict of Nantes. Every Reformed church was placed in an accusatory posture and had to appear before the *commission* to justify its existence. Representatives of the Catholic Church argued almost systematically for the closure of Reformed churches.[8] The Protestant city of Nîmes was looked at as a new Geneva and mountain communities had remained places of Huguenot concentrations. Dozens of churches were forcibly closed in Bas-Languedoc and the Cévennes. At the time, there were about one hundred-forty thousand Protestants, or *"religionnaires"* as they were called in the two provinces. As a result of protests against measures enacted to destabilize churches, Protestants were forbidden to correspond between provinces in order to prevent any collective protestation.[9]

6. Daireaux, "Louis XIV et les protestants normands," 125–26.

7. Janzé, *Les Huguenots*, §209.

8. Daireaux, "Louis XIV et les protestants normands," 126–27.

9. Bost, *Prédicants Protestants*, 6–7.

The French clergy worked feverishly to undermine the Edict of Nantes piece by piece. The clergy assembled every five years and used these occasions to inflame the king's zeal. They congratulated the king in 1665 for leveling the "synagogues of Satan" and stigmatized the freedom of conscience. They requested measures so drastic that the king, once having granted them, often delayed their execution. A decree in October 1665 authorized children to separate from their parents and embrace Catholicism, boys at the age of fourteen, girls at twelve. It was sufficient that a child make the sign of the cross, kiss a medal, or manifest the desire to enter a church to justify the removal of children from their family. In 1670, the clergy expressed their consternation that the Huguenots claimed equality with the Catholic religion. As a result, Catholics were forbidden to convert to Protestantism and Protestant converts to Catholicism were forbidden to return to their former religion. In 1675, the clergy brought new complaints and gave the king a large sum of money to help persuade him of the justice of their cause. In 1676 Louis XIV followed Louis XIII in providing funds (caisse de conversion) to obtain conversions with the amount paid depending on the status of the converted. Beginning in 1679 the conflict became more bitter. The legal insecurity of the 1660s and 1670s was replaced by measures to dismantle the Protestant churches.[10] Louis XIV no longer cunningly sought to undermine the Edict of Nantes, but was determined to bypass it. The clergy assembled in 1680 and praised the king for demolishing Protestant temples and excluding Huguenots from civil and military posts. Soon after the king unleashed the ferocious *dragonnades* on a population constrained to lodge *dragons* in Protestant homes in order to accelerate conversions. The king's soldiers terrorized Protestants and sought forced conversions, and the physical intimidation was often connected to financial incentives. Protestants who agreed to convert were exempt from lodging the *dragons* for a designated period. The prohibitions were multiplied—Huguenots were forbidden to congregate outside their authorized places of worship and permitted to worship only at specific times; they were forbidden to sing the Psalms during worship; pastors were forbidden to stay in one place for more than three years; marriages between Catholics and Protestants were forbidden; ceremonies of baptism or marriages were limited to twelve persons; burials were forbidden during the day and only ten persons allowed to gather; pastors were forbidden to criticize the Catholic Church in any way; and they were forbidden to receive new converts into churches

10. Daireaux, "Louis XIV et les protestants normands," 127.

under threat of banishment and confiscation of property for the pastor and closing the church to the people. Those who were hospitalized were pressured to convert and visited by magistrates to obtain their abjuration. Most Protestant schools were closed and Huguenot parents were not allowed to send their sons abroad for studies. Little by little the Huguenots lost virtually all the rights granted by the Edict of Nantes.[11]

The situation changed profoundly in 1684 with intensified repression and demolition of temples. In January 1685, the remaining Protestants addressed their final petition to the king. He had been persuaded by the clergy that with the harsh methods employed, the practice of Reformed worship had diminished to the point where few Huguenots were left in France. Now he discovered otherwise and the clergy lay the blame on the obstinacy of the Protestants and the inability of priests to combat the heresy. In addition, the new converts to Catholicism were exonerated from taxes at the expense of Catholics of long date. Finally, Louis XIV yielded to the clergy's pressure to obtain the Revocation of the Edict of Nantes on October 18, 1685, also known as the Edict of Fontainebleau. The date marks the zenith of this great king; it also signaled the beginning of crises leading to his demise in his vain attempts to rid the kingdom of heretics.[12] The king's subjects were compelled to adopt the religion of the one who ruled by divine right, but contrary to what other European sovereigns had done, he would not allow those who refused conversion to emigrate. This was an explicit denial of the freedom of conscience and the logical outcome of absolute monarchism. Protestant worship was forbidden in France and the edict led once again to the illegal departure of thousands of French Protestants.[13]

In a matter of only a few years, the Protestant situation in France was radically and perilously reversed. The Reformation had been solidly rooted in many provinces in the middle of the seventeenth century. Reformed churches had benefitted greatly from favorable conditions created by the Edict of Nantes. Churches and synods had been well organized, led by quality leaders, and demonstrated loyalty toward royal power. By 1685, the most prominent temples had been demolished, the Protestant numbers reduced, and thousands exiled. Armed resistance in response to persecution would once again shortly become the order of the day.[14]

11. Stéphan, *L'Épopée huguenote*, 226–29.

12. Stéphan, *L'Épopée huguenote*, 236–38.

13. De Montclos, *Histoire religieuse*, 69.

14. Daireaux, "Louis XIV et les protestants normands," 129.

ARTICLES OF REVOCATION

The articles of the Edict of Revocation reveal the drastic measures under-taken to extirpate the Protestant religion in France. The edict's preamble stated that since the majority of R.P.R. (*religion prétendue réformée*) ad-herents had embraced Catholicism, there was no longer any need for the Edict of Nantes. Once the public exercise of Protestant church services was abolished, legally there were no more Protestants in France. Article one or-dered the demolition of Protestant temples. Articles two and three forbade all religious assemblies with the threat of prison. Articles four, five, and six ordered the expulsion within fifteen days of all Protestant pastors who refused to convert to Catholicism and the inducement of lifetime pensions for those who converted. Article seven outlawed Protestant schools. Article eight obliged all infants to be baptized into the Catholic Church and receive religious instruction from village priests. Articles nine and ten ordered the confiscation of possessions of those who already emigrated unless they re-turned within a specified period, and forbade Protestant emigration under the threat of galleys for the men and imprisonment for the women. Article eleven stipulated punishment for new converts who relapsed into heresy in refusing the sacraments of the Church. Article twelve granted the right to remain in the kingdom to the not-yet-enlightened R.P.R. conditioned by the interdiction of assemblies for worship or prayer. Various methods were utilized to pressure Protestants to convert. The Church opened centers of conversion (*maisons de conversion*) and continued to place mounted *drag-ons* in Huguenot homes to ensure their attendance at mass and to force conversions. In effect, the Edict of Revocation forced hundreds of thou-sands of dissidents to convert to the prince's religion without allowing them the liberty to leave the territory.[15]

The fear of the *dragons* led to waves of conversions among entire vil-lages and accelerated the disappearance of the R.P.R. In only a few months, hundreds of thousands of Protestants converted to Catholicism. Those who converted were called N.C. (*nouveaux convertis or nouveaux catholiques*) and placed under strict surveillance. In the last moments of life, the refusal of extreme unction could lead to their bodies being dragged in the streets, the confiscation of all their possessions, and the loss of any inheritance for their families. It has been estimated that from 1685 to 1715 over two hundred thousand Protestants escaped and emigrated to places of refuge

---

15. Carbonnier-Burkard, *La révolte des Camisards,* 17–19.

including Geneva, England, Germany, and Holland. Among them were soldiers, sailors, magistrates, intellectuals, merchants, and craftsmen. Many believe that to some degree this exodus impoverished France and enriched her neighbors.[16] Louis XIV's strict application of the Edict of Nantes before the Revocation had already led many Reformed believers to emigrate to places where they could practice their faith. This was done in spite of edicts in 1669 and 1682 prohibiting Protestant emigration. The Revocation, which prohibited both the exercise of the Protestant religion and departure to other countries, accelerated these illegal departures. An exception was made for ministers who were given the chance to leave the country under strict conditions. Of the approximately seven hundred eighty pastors still in France in 1685, six hundred twenty left in exile and one hundred sixty recanted, among which some later renounced their abjuration. For all others, the prohibition to emigrate was absolute.[17]

During the sixteenth-century Wars of Religion, Catholics and Protestants killed each other but did not forcibly convert others. The conversion of Protestants was considered the result of divine intervention and not a result of moral or physical violence from the State or Church. In most of the edicts or treaties of pacification, a similar formula is found—"while waiting for it to please God to reunite all our subjects with our Catholic Church." Under Louis XIV a century later, the persistence of a Protestant presence led the government to employ violence and bribes to convert Protestants. A minority religious population was neither allowed to emigrate nor live in tranquility. With their pastors gone, the Huguenots took up arms and gathered secretly in spite of a royal decree which in July 1686 threatened the sentence of death to all subjects of the kingdom found by the king's troops in clandestine assemblies.[18]

The Revocation reestablished the union of the throne and altar leading to the persecution of the Huguenots who had valiantly fought for the principle of freedom of conscience. The Catholic Church welcomed the Revocation, re-aligned itself with the Royal State, and continued the Counter-Reformation with the rejection of religious liberty and freedom of thought.[19] There were also material benefits for the monarchy in revoking the Edict of Nantes. Before the reign of Louis XIV, Anne d'Autriche

16. Stéphan, *L'Épopée huguenote*, 237.

17. Carbonnier-Burkard, *La révolte des Camisards*, 20–23.

18. Carbonnier-Burkard, *La révolte des Camisards*, 31.

19. Gaillard, "L'invention de la laïcité," 21–22.

lived lavishly and had accorded privileges and monopolies to her admirers and sycophants. The debts she incurred weighed heavily on court finances. Louis XIV inherited and added to those debts. The Revocation provided an opportunity for the royal court to satisfy its debts and to continue in sumptuous debauchery. Over six hundred Protestant temples were destroyed. Their contents were originally destined for distribution to Catholic hospitals and other charitable works. The royal court eyed these treasures and the Jesuits decided that the plunder would go to the king rather than to hospitals. In return, the king favored and recompensed with the spoils those who participated in confiscations. The possessions of individuals were soon targeted as prey for distribution among the king's loyalists, religious and otherwise. With the population decimated by periodic famines and dying of hunger, Louis XIV left the royal place at the Louvre in Paris and settled at Versailles in 1682 surrounded by his court. Versailles, originally a hunting lodge built under Louis XIII, became his principal residence. It was expanded and embellished at exorbitant cost, the ostentatious symbol of his power and influence in Europe. There he and his courtesans reveled in profligate and sumptuous living off the confiscation of possessions from the living and the dead. Counted among the beneficiaries were abbots and bishops of the Church, unashamed to profit from the despoliation of helpless Protestants, now fugitives and exiles.[20]

Those who fled before and after the Revocation became the "second Refuge" in joining those who had left in the sixteenth century. Forty percent of Protestants in northern provinces of the kingdom crossed the borders to find safety, while only 16 percent in the Midi and 2 percent in the Cévennes fled France. The majority of those who remained, two-thirds of Reformed believers, did not convert to Catholicism and began to organize themselves, first in small groups then in large assemblies in out-of-the-way places.[21] They were cut down; they were not destroyed. Their regions were delivered to fire and sword and considered unworthy of pity. As in the past, the Huguenots were subjects of calumny for their collusion with foreign powers. True, they sought outside assistance from those sympathetic to the Protestant faith in their combat against a government which had conspired for centuries with foreign powers to exterminate them. In reality, regardless of their alliances and appeals for foreign assistance, the simple fact of

20. Janzé, *Les Huguenots*, §623.

21. Garrisson, *Histoire des protestants*, 193–95.

preaching in violation of royal edicts and gathering in secret places for worship was sufficient to condemn them to death.[22]

CHURCH OF THE DESERT

After the Revocation, the persecuted Huguenots became "metaphoric Hebrews." Their prophets and military leaders adopted names associated with the Jewish people of the Old Testament—*Josué* Janavel, *Abraham* Mazel, *Salomon* Couderic, *Élie* Marion, among others. Their most famous clandestine preacher, Claude Brousson (1647–1698) entitled his collection of sermons "*La manne mystique du Désert*." The "Church of the Desert" recalled the wilderness wanderings of the children of Israel after their exodus from Egyptian bondage, and came to designate a period when Reformed religion was outlawed with echoes of the Exodus and liberation of the people of God from the hand of Pharoah. The Huguenots saw themselves as a wandering people on a journey toward the promised land without a secure earthly dwelling place. They worshipped in secret, wandering in the woods and savage places of the Cévennes and Vivarais. Minority Protestants and minority Jews in fact had a shared experience of banishment, deprivation, and persecution. Some Huguenots recognized this parallel experience and destiny and perceived that it was time to end religious intolerance.[23]

For Catholic historians, the prophets and preachers of the Cévennes were seditious rebels working hand-in-hand with France's enemies and seeking to deliver the province to foreign powers. Therefore, punishment was meted out to criminals of the State who were unworthy of pity and undeserving to be considered martyrs by their coreligionists. Protestant historians largely reject this accusation and instead see in it an odious slander to tarnish the memory of the persecuted. The return of men like Claude Brousson and François Vivent (1664–1692) to the Cévennes in 1689 was primarily for the consolation of their cruelly persecuted brothers and to address errors that had arisen in the absence of pastors. Brousson had self-exiled to Geneva and Lausanne, then returned to France to preach, to distribute his sermons, and to organize clandestine gatherings at night. Vivent had refused to abjure in 1685 and was hunted down, then finally authorized to leave the country in 1687, and found refuge first in Holland, then in Switzerland. These men were united in their desire to reestablish

22. Bost, *Prédicants Protestants*, x.

23. Cabanel, "Au Miroir," 487–88.

Protestant worship and in their conviction that a state religion was not in conformity to biblical teachings. They wanted to avoid the annihilation of the Protestant religion and encouraged believers to remain steadfast. Upon their return to France, they addressed what has been called a "prophetic epidemic" which was rampant in regions deserted by pastors and savaged by repression.[24]

Vivent, Brousson, and their companions unquestionably returned to France to awaken the piety and zeal of new converts, but also to join the coalition of William of Orange (1650–1702) to war against the oppressor Louis XIV in their quest for liberty, justice, and the reestablishment of the Edict of Nantes. They returned to the Cévennes to stir up the population and confront Louis XIV with a formidable insurrection, with promises of support from England, Switzerland, and Holland. As attested in letters written by Pierre Jurieu (1637–1713), Brousson, and others, one thing becomes clear. The persecuted church sought above all the freedom of conscience, the freedom to practice their religion without interference from the State and the established Church. This freedom had been offered to them under Henri IV and snatched away by the despot Louis XIV. Both Brousson and Vivent became martyrs for the great cause of freedom of religion; Vivent was killed in a cave defending himself on February 19, 1692; Brousson was executed at Montpellier on November 4, 1698.[25] When we remember the sufferings of the victims of intolerance, many of whom had loved ones in dungeons or prisoners on the king's galley ships, we better understand any acts of desperation, even those acts which shock our sensibilities today. Ultimately, the greater part of the blame is on the persecutors. The persecuted Protestant minority had unceasingly affirmed their loyalty to the throne as subjects and their duty to God as Christians. If there was a change in sentiments which led to exasperation and extreme measures, the fault lies squarely on the Revocation. The result was the destruction of Protestant churches, the flock scattered, families torn apart, pastors exiled, and Christians hunted down as criminals.[26]

In the absence of pastors, prophets and prophetesses proliferated in Dauphiné, in Vivarais, and especially in the Cévennes. In the beginning, these self-appointed leaders preached the gospel, exhorted to repentance, and made promises of freedom. In time, claiming inspiration of the Spirit

24. Krumenacker, *Marie Durand*, 79.
25. Stéphan, *L'Épopée huguenote*, 265.
26. Bost, *Prédicants Protestants*, ix–xi.

and nourished by the Old Testament, many fell into mystical trances and preached revolt. Pastors in general disapproved of their activities and attributed it to the lack of spiritual guides.[27] We should not yield, however, to the temptation to see this prophetism as merely a mental aberration. Apart from the disconcerting forms associated with the prophecies, the content of the messages was most often in continuity with the preaching of the seventeenth century. This prophetic preaching evoked realties well known to the listeners and brought joy and confidence to the afflicted Huguenot people. Early manifestations of prophetism were peaceful until 1702. Following increasing arrests and executions, the prophetic message changed into a call to holy wars and armed resistance to punish the infidels.[28]

WAR OF THE CAMISARDS

André Chamson's *Suite Camisarde* presents the Revocation of the Edict of Nantes as a foundational event which sheds light on the religious, regional, and historic collective memory of the Cévenol region of France and the War of the Camisards. The war was triggered by Louis XIV's intention to impose one law and one faith on the kingdom, and tore apart the Cévennes from 1702 to 1705. The Camisards fought to defend and to reclaim their religious rights obtained with the Edict of Nantes in 1598. Above all they fought for the freedom of conscience to freely worship the God of their religion. Thousands of men were imprisoned, deported, sent to the galleys, tortured, and more than five hundred villages suffered the great burning (*le grand brûlement*).[29] The origin of the word "Camisard" as a description for Cévenol insurgents is disputed. According to some, they owe their name to the white shirt they wore over their clothing in order to be recognized among themselves.[30] Others see a reference to an old word "*camisade*" (night attack) or "*camin*" in patois referring to paths along mountain ridges.[31] Their numbers at any one time rarely exceeded one thousand men with a total of approximately seven to ten thousand men engaged in combat in the years 1700–1705. Over 50 percent were younger than twenty-five years old, mostly from rural or semi-rural regions. Over two-thirds were artisans

27. Stéphan, *L'Épopée huguenote*, 263–64.

28. Garrison, *Histoire des protestants*, 199.

29. Chamson, *Suite Camisarde*, iii.

30. *Nouveau Petit Robert*, 335.

31. Stéphan, *L'Épopée huguenote*, 266.

in textile; one-third were shepherds or farmers. The Protestant nobility was largely absent, while some were active in the repression of their co-religionaries. The wives and sisters of the Camisards followed the troops, and at times wielded the sword.[32]

The war had its beginning in July 1702 when the prophet Pierre Séguier, called Esprit Séguier, declared during an assembly that the Spirit had called him to liberate prisoners arrested and tortured by the abbot of Chaila at Pont-de-Montvert. Accompanied by Abraham Mazel, Séguier and forty men marched all night and surrounded the presbytery. They forced open the doors, freed the prisoners, killed the abbot, and set the edifice on fire. Emboldened by their success, they set fire to two churches and killed eleven Catholics. Three of the attackers were captured and tortured, Séguier among them, who was burned at the stake at Pont-de-Montvert. [33] Early on the Camisards wreaked havoc throughout the Cévennes under the leadership of Abraham Mazel, Gédéon Laporte, Jean Cavalier, and Salomon Couderc. They practiced the Old Testament law of the talion, destroyed churches in response to their temples burned down, and put fear in village priests who sought refuge in cities. During their first military encounter in September 1702, Laporte and Cavalier faced off against soldiers led by Captain Poul. A month later, Laporte and several of his men were surprised in a ravine and killed, their heads exposed on the bridge of Anduze as a warning to the insurgents.[34] Laporte's nephew Pierre Laporte, later known as Rolland, and Cavalier, sheep castrator and shepherd respectively, led small groups of poorly armed peasants for two years in guerrilla warfare against the king's troops. The success of the Camisards was partly due to their knowledge of the rugged countryside with its woods, ravines, and caves. They had the complicity of newly-converted Catholics and were feared by other Catholics. They held frequent worship gatherings and sang Psalm 68 "*Que Dieu se montre*" (Let God arise) before attacking the enemy with fury. The royal troops often fled at the first notes intoned of the Camisard hymn.[35] A letter addressed to the Count Broglie by the rebels in December 1702 explained their demands. They wrote that they simply wanted the freedoms purchased with the blood of their ancestors and that they were prepared to die rather than renounce their beliefs. Because the edicts of the king had deprived

32. Carbonnier-Burkard, *La révolte des Camisards*, 55–56.
33. Stéphan, *L'Épopée huguenote*, 265.
34. Carbonnier-Burkard, *La révolte des Camisards*, 60–61.
35. Stéphan, *L'Épopée huguenote*, 267–69.

them of their right of public assembly to worship, they had withdrawn into the mountains and caves. They deplored the massacres committed by agents of the Catholic Church and the cruelty of the measures against them. They expressed their confidence that the God of mercy had poured out his Spirit on them according to the promise of the prophet Joel and they were constrained to now offer their bodies and possessions in sacrifice for the holy gospel and spill their blood for this just cause. The following month, Broglie pursued Catinat and Ravenel near Nîmes with three companies of *dragons* where he was defeated and Captain Poul killed in battle.[36]

Skirmishes and punitive expeditions dragged on in the early months of 1703. A promise of amnesty was made in June 1703 for those who laid down their arms, and was interpreted by the Camisards as a sign of weakness. Cévenols whose homes had been destroyed swelled the ranks of the Camisards. The combats continued with both resounding victories and stinging defeats for the insurgents. In March, the united troops of Rolland and Cavalier were soundly defeated at Pompignan. The *nouveaux convertis* of Mialet and Saumane, suspected of aiding and abetting the Camisards, were deported to Perpignan.[37] There were further attempts to depopulate the Hautes-Cévennes through the methodic destruction of villages, followed by reprisals from Rolland against Catholic villages and Camisard victories led by Cavalier. Finally, Louis XIV sent Marshal de Villars to Languedoc as a replacement for the Marshal de Montrevel with assurances from the king of limited freedoms and the repudiation of past excesses. This new proposal led to defections among the Camisards and Cavalier himself proposed negotiations. He was seduced by Villars' offer, extended without awaiting the king's consent, to form a regiment of Camisards of which he would be colonel, and also accepted a verbal promise of freedom of conscience. The king had no intention of having a regiment of Camisards among his troops, and Cavalier and one hundred of his men were escorted by the king's soldiers from the province with promises unfulfilled, never to return. The remaining Camisards who wanted places of worship in the Cévennes considered Cavalier a traitor. They banded together with Rolland who refused to surrender and awaited assistance from his allies. He was betrayed by a young cousin and delivered to Bâville, who governed Languedoc from 1695 to 1718.[38] Trapped in the chateau of Castelnau-

---

36. Carbonnier-Burkard, *La révolte des Camisards*, 63–66.

37. Carbonnier-Burkard, *La révolte des Camisards*, 70.

38. Armogathe and Joutard, "Bâville et la guerre des camisards," 44.

Valence, Rolland was shot to death on August 14, 1704 while attempting to flee, his cadaver dragged through the streets of Nîmes and his five companions executed. After Rolland's death the Camisards were demoralized. One by one their leaders surrendered and were allowed to leave the kingdom for Switzerland. There was one final attempt at revolt in the spring of 1705, but the conspiracy was discovered and the perpetrators severely punished. Several of Cavalier's and Rolland's men were seized and executed at Nîmes. Castanet was captured and died on the rack before ten thousand spectators at Montpellier. He addressed his final words to the executioner concerning the priests who sought his repentance: "*Retirez de moi ces sauterelles du puits de l'abîme*" (Remove from me these locusts from the bottomless pit). After a failed kidnapping attempt, Catinat and Ravenal were captured and executed at Nîmes, dressed in shirts covered with sulfur and burned at the stake. Only Mazel remained, who after escaping from prison attempted an insurrection in Vivarais. He and sixty peasants resisted one year against the royal troops before his betrayal and death on October 7, 1710. His companions were hanged or put to death on the rack. Thus ended the War of the Camisards and the last war of religion. This final war lasted two years and was limited to the province of Languedoc. The uprising of poor peasants against one of the most powerful European kings appeared to have both heroic and foolish aspects. The longevity of the Camisard epic is sustained by the novelty of their combat and sacrifice. They fought in spite of the odds against them, and lived and died with the conviction that their consciences must be free. The organizers of the "Church of the Desert" after the death of Louis XIV in 1715 remembered the immense sacrifices of the Camisards.[39]

The power of the Church and the exclusion and exile of tens of thousands of Protestants would harden antagonisms for the next century. Louis XIV, in spite of his boast of reducing the number of Huguenots from nine hundred thousand to fifteen thousand, had failed to destroy the Reformation in France, and the persecution and exile of Huguenots blessed other nations in extending Reformed teachings and sending Huguenots throughout the world to places of refuge. Those exiled included groups of convicts for the faith who had spent thirty years on the king's galleys and were liberated in 1713 and 1714 under orders to leave the kingdom without delay. This was not a general freedom of all Protestant galley slaves and the last

---

39. Stéphan, *L'Épopée huguenote*, 270–73; Miquel, *Guerres de religion*, 507–11.

prisoners on the king's galleys were finally released in 1775 shortly before the French Revolution.[40]

HUGUENOT HEROES

Joutard affirms that France seems to have largely forgotten the struggle of the Huguenots. Outside the world of Protestantism there are few who know the names of Antoine Court and Marie Durand. Or they consider the Protestant question settled with the death of Louis XIV.[41] Of the innumerable heroes and heroines following the War of the Camisards, we look at these two representatives whose exploits are remarkable for their faith and valor during a long and sorrowful period in French history. Many others have had their stories told; many have remained nameless in the shadows known only to God. They were treated as treasonous criminals and the offscouring of society for the crime of practicing their faith. In fact, they were betrayed by their government which revoked an edict that had been perpetual and irrevocable. These two individuals came on the scene after the War of the Camisards. Free from entanglement in foreign wars, Louis XIV issued a new declaration a few months before his death stating that residence in the kingdom was a sign of catholicity. From this date on all the subjects of the king were also subjects of the Catholic Church.[42]

Antoine Court

On August 21, 1715, Antoine Court, only twenty years old, gathered several people to lay new foundations for French reformed churches. As a child he had accompanied his mother to assemblies where prophetesses had replaced exiled pastors. Following the non-realization of prophesies, he broke with the prophetism, rejected the violence associated with the Camisards, and fought against the consequences of the Revocation.[43] Just days before the death of Louis XIV, the most powerful monarch of Europe, who lay in agony on his deathbed and died ten days later on September 1, 1715, Court had the audacity to constitute the first synod of the "Desert" and replant the

40. Whelan, "Enfin libres!" 285–86.
41. Joutard, "Antoine Court," 80.
42. Carbonnier-Burkard, *La révolte des Camisards*, 95.
43. Garrisson, *Histoire des protestants*, 203.

church which Louis XIV sought to destroy.[44] His death sparked great hope among the Huguenots for the reestablishment of the Edict of Nantes. Their hope did not long survive. Shortly after, a young preacher, Étienne Arnaud, was arrested. Court opposed a project to liberate Arnaud who was put to death by hanging at Alès on January 22, 1718 in the presence of a large crowd. His death had a great impact on Protestants beyond the Cévennes region and a martyr was born. Two years later, in the region of Nîmes, another assembly was called with Court and other leaders of the "Church of the Desert." The king's troops intervened, Court escaped, but fifty others were arrested including an eighty-year-old man. As an example, twenty men were sentenced to the galleys for life. They were transported through France to La Rochelle where they were liberated by Protestant authorities and exiled to England.[45] Worse yet, in 1724 a royal declaration by Louis XV reinstituted the Edict of Revocation in a single text declaring France a Catholic nation. Protestants were considered "relapsed," a word used for Protestant converts to Catholicism (*nouveaux convertis*) and subject to harsh penalties. Although the royal decree was applied sporadically and never consistently throughout the kingdom, there was great consternation among Protestants. Submission was unthinkable, yet further emigration might announce the end of French Protestantism, and armed revolt would annul the decision ten years earlier when Protestants had renounced violence. Their response had two parts. On one hand, they planned to organize public gatherings which would disperse at the announcement of the arrival of troops. On the other hand, they would refuse to participate in Catholic ceremonies, particularly baptism, marriage, and extreme unction. It fell to Antoine Court at a synod in 1725 to convince the faithful who continued to suffer persecution of the wisdom of these actions. In his speech he recalled the origin of their suffering under Louis XIV and God's faithfulness in raising up his servants to sustain his people. In his writings Court addressed what he believed the greatest problem in reorganizing Reformed churches—the War of the Camisards. At that time, violence and prophetic inspiration were brought together and resulted in atrocities such as the murder of the abbot of Chaila which had marked the beginning of the Wars of the Camisards.[46] Court's strategy was based on a rupture from violence and prophetic inspiration. Early on in his life, although not a Camisard,

44. Stéphan, *L'Épopée huguenote*, 275.

45. Joutard, "Antoine Court," 75–76.

46. Garrisson, *Histoire des protestants*, 199.

he was an accomplice and admitted to writing letters to priests in which he threatened a new uprising if persecution continued. He separated from those who claimed prophetic inspiration yet remained surrounded by many who had participated in the War of the Camisards. He convinced his companions to separate from the violence and from those who claimed prophetic inspiration for their actions. Yet many Huguenots were sensitive to the existence of continuity between the periods of armed resistance and pacifism, and conversion to nonviolent resistance was difficult for many who had experienced systematic persecution.[47]

In his book, *Histoire des troubles des Cévennes*, Court sought to reconcile these different periods and showed how the excesses of intolerance and the dearth of spiritual leadership contributed to the impossibility of controlling processes which led to violence instigated by the prophetic utterances of Camisard leaders. He likewise insisted that the situation following the rebellion influenced his strategy of nonviolence which was more consistent with evangelical principles. Yet others claim Court was unable to admit that the threat of insurrection often stopped the authorities from exercising harsh repression. To his opponents, Court remained prisoner of a mindset which accorded undeserved reverence to the monarchy. Court found himself confronted by questions which go beyond his time and resonate in the twenty-first century. In the defense of a just cause, is there an impervious boundary between violence and nonviolence? In extreme situations, how do we articulate and differentiate between legality and legitimacy? Even if Court did not always have the right response, he asked the right questions for the benefit of a minority defending their faith, their values, and their culture.[48] Although he adopted a strategy of non-violence and submission to political authority, his objective remained the same as the Camisards'— obtain the freedom of conscience, the freedom to be born, to live, and to die outside of the Catholic Church. The tolerance which eventually gained ground in Languedoc after the renewal of persecution from 1745 to 1755 undoubtably was the result of Court's position as well as the fear of a new Camisard uprising.[49]

47. Joutard, "Antoine Court," 76.
48. Joutard, "Antoine Court," 78–79.
49. Carbonnier-Burkard, *La révolte des Camisards,* 96.

Marie Durand

Of the Protestant women who exhibited devotion and courage in the struggle for truth and the freedom of conscience, Marie Durand stands apart. She is not widely known outside of French Protestantism. She was the daughter of Étienne and Claudine Gamonet, a deeply Protestant couple forcefully converted to Catholicism following the Revocation in 1685. The Gamonets' children were compelled to attend Mass and catechism, and yet received a clandestine Protestant instruction. Marie had an older brother, Pierre, who at the age of sixteen assisted the leaders when the Reformed Church reorganized in 1715. He was later consecrated to the ministry in 1726. On January 29, 1719, Étienne was arrested by the king's soldiers during a secret worship service at which Pierre was preaching. Pierre escaped to Switzerland, his mother Claudine was imprisoned at the citadel of Montpellier, and their home destroyed.[50] Pierre later returned to France to preach and married the sister of a friend who had been condemned to the king's galleys. The authorities again arrested Pierre's father in 1729, who remained imprisoned for fourteen years before being released, and died in 1749 at the age of ninety-two. Marie, at the age of fifteen or sixteen, against the advice of her brother Pierre, married Mathieu Serre in 1730, a man twenty-five years her senior. Shortly after their secret marriage both Marie and Mathieu were arrested. Mathieu was taken to the fort of Brescou and released twenty years later. Marie was imprisoned in the Tower of Constance at Aigues-Mortes in southern France. Since 1720 the Tower had been reserved for women and for children born to prisoners. When Marie arrived, she joined twenty-eight women, mostly prophetesses. Marie, imprisoned for being the sister of a pastor, spent thirty-eight years there in unimaginable, inhumane conditions. Apart from children born there, she was the youngest captive. In spite of the execution of her brother Pierre in 1732, she rose to lead the other women, and wrote letters for herself and for the other women to request help or to stay in contact with their families. These letters, of which about fifty have been found, have contributed to her renown in providing detailed information about life in the Tower of Constance and the faith of the prisoners. Marie was liberated April 14, 1768 and returned to her natal village, Bouschet-de-Pranles where she died in 1776, aged and infirm beyond her years. Her suffering for the faith and her

---

50. Krumenacker, *Marie Durand*, 80.

refusal to recant her belief serve as a reminder of the price paid by those who resisted State and Church coercion.[51]

REVOCATION AND REFUGEES

At the end of the seventeenth century, the historian Élie Benoist in his *Histoire de l'édit de Nantes*, spoke of one million refugees; Voltaire of eight hundred thousand; Antoine Court of two million; much later Alfred Rébelliau, in his *Histoire de la France*, arrived at one million. These figures are astonishing taking into consideration that Protestants numbered around eight hundred thousand at the time of the Revocation. The real number appears to be 135,000–180,000 refugees from 1680 to the end of the century.[52] Whatever the number of refugees might be there was some loss to France in her financial, economic, technological, military and cultural genius. In all likelihood, however, the French economy was developed to the point that a small percentage of exiles did not profoundly affect it although the flight of refugees certainly enriched other nations and challenged France's economic and military dominance.[53] Fleeing Huguenots found a welcome in many Protestant cities and nations. As an example, less than a month after the Revocation, the Edict of Potsdam under Frederick William, Elector of Brandenburg and Duke of Prussia, encouraged Huguenot refugees to relocate to Brandenburg and accorded to them the same rights and privileges as those born there.[54] The losses to France following the Revocation went beyond the loss of money and people. As fragile and complicated as the peace had been since 1598, the societal benefits were real in the doubling of institutions such as schools, commerces, and even cemeteries. When Louis XIV began to shrink the Protestant space, the gains were sacrificed and substituted with the mirage of unity. And France lost any hope of peaceful coexistence. The Huguenots' welcome by other nations was real but had its share of pragmatism, xenophobia, and hardship.[55]

Cabanel speaks of a "façade of unity" offered by the Revocation. By means of state violence, France falsely believed she had rediscovered spiritual unity. Religious leaders justified their actions in appealing to

51. Krumenacker, *Marie Durand*, 81–82; Kirschleger, "Mon âme est en liberté," 569.

52. Cabanel, "Enchanter, désenchanter l'histoire," 409–10.

53. Garrisson, *Histoire des protestants*, 194.

54. Cabanel, "Enchanter, désenchanter l'histoire," 412.

55. Cabanel, "Enchanter, désenchanter l'histoire," 414.

Augustine's commentary on the master sending his servant to invite people to a feast. Those who did not respond to the invitation should be compelled (*compelle intrare*) to enter the Church. Cabanel finds a connection between Church terror of 1685 and State terror of 1793 in the battle against freedom of conscience. In 1685 Louis XIV considered as outlaws the remaining faithful of the cursed Huguenots. One hundred years later the French monarchy and the French clergy paid dearly for their tyranny. The victors of the Revocation became the victims of the Revolution. The king of France and his family were massacred by their subjects and priests were forced into exile, happy to find refuge among the descendants of those whom their predecessors had persecuted. And through violence another façade of unity was inaugurated.[56]

The religious persecution of the Huguenots following the Revocation of the Edict of Nantes has made them the representatives of the great cause of the freedom of conscience. They held to this sacred freedom which had been wrested from them with violence and with the most perfidious methods. Their repeated requests for justice, their plaintive pleas for mercy, and their oaths of allegiance to the Crown, all failed at the foot of the throne of despots. Louis XIV, as an instrument of the Catholic Church, employed odious schemes of corruption and violence against the Huguenots—confiscation, imprisonment, exile, condemnation as king's galley slaves, the rack, the gallows, and the stake—in order to give the appearance of a general conversion of the Huguenots to the Catholic Church. His successors multiplied the kidnapping of children and populated the prisons and the galleys for the sole crime of gathering to worship God in their own manner. More than a million French were deprived of the right to marry, to baptize their children, and bury their dead without the consent of the Catholic Church which held the official registers of civil status. Couples who married in the wilderness were considered living in sin and their offspring as bastards. Why? Because the Catholic Church did not recognize marriage outside of the Church.[57] Only in 1787 with the Edict of Toleration would French Protestants be considered fully French with the right to marry before a civil official, register the birth of their children, and bury their dead. They still were merely "tolerated" and did not enjoy full religious rights and freedom. They could neither worship publicly nor sing or pray when accompanying their dead in funeral processions. They could not become professors or

56. Cabanel, "Enchanter, désenchanter l'histoire," 415.

57. Janzé, *Les Huguenots*, §3.

judges. Full recognition for Protestants as truly and legally French would come only with the much-maligned French Revolution in 1789.

Chapter 8

The French Revolution

THE FRENCH REVOLUTION WAS more than an event. It was a series of events which played out for a tumultuous decade. The period extends from 1789 to 1799 with the introduction of a constitutional monarchy, the inception of the disestablishment of the official and dominant Church, and the inauguration of a new political order. The arrival of the Revolution broke with the model of governance (*Ancien Régime*) with its societal divisions and the mingling of Church and State in the affairs of the citizenry. The absolute monarchy legitimated by divine right was replaced by the sovereignty of the people. The atrocities of the Revolution and the Reign of Terror which followed are well known and in hindsight rightly criticized. During the Terror there was a brutal fight against persons and possessions led by proconsuls who not only preyed on Catholicism but also on Protestantism and Judaism.[1] The removal of the Catholic Church from public influence and the overthrow of the monarchy were among the objectives achieved by the Revolution. The tithe, the Church's principal source of revenue, was eliminated in August 1789 in the name of fiscal justice. The Civil Clergy Constitution of 1790, which nationalized French Catholicism, was approved by Louis XVI. Tolerance was granted to non-Catholics and ecclesiastical properties were nationalized. The number of bishops was reduced. Priests and bishops were elected by districts and departments respectively and both became civil servants remunerated by the State. Pope Pius VI (1717–1799) condemned this action and priests were divided between those who swore

---

1. De Montclos, *Histoire religieuse*, 87.

loyalty to the Republic and those who looked to Rome for guidance. Persecution and division followed.[2]

ROAD TO REVOLUTION

Although the differences between the political French Revolution and the religious Reformation are more numerous than their similarities, there is commonality in their reactionary thinking, in a yearning for change, and the Reformation might be seen as a precursor of the Revolution. For both in the end, there was political and religious upheaval and long-term implications for society which reverberate to our day. Societal and religious unrest are often associated, and the pre-revolutionary social hierarchy in France sheds light on conditions which contributed to discontent and turbulence which fed revolutionary flames.[3] Clergy and nobility were largely exonerated from the crushing taxes imposed on the peasantry. Added to the contempt felt by the peasants was their exclusion from the ranks of military officers. Beginning with the Reformation, the Huguenots clashed with the Church, the first privileged order of the State, which had no intention of relinquishing power and prestige. The monarchy reached its zenith under Louis XIV where the king remained the living symbol of a system in which the Catholic Church was the state religion. It was no surprise that kings and the Church declared war on the Protestants who threatened the status quo.[4]

After Henri IV signed the compromise of the Edict of Nantes to restore civil peace, Louis XIII and Louis XIV emptied the edict of its substance before its revocation. They were determined that Protestants should perish and refused to surrender the principles of a monarchy of divine right. The monarchy, even in decline, in the face of mounting public opinion, could not deny itself. Protestants had chosen another religion and had lost any claim to have a part in the State, in spite of their submission to the Crown.[5] Following the Revocation and War of the Camisards, Protestantism won ground throughout the kingdom and new clandestine churches were established. A period of relative calm was observed until persecution recommenced in 1732. Men and women surprised at secret gatherings were still

2. Gaillard, "L'invention de la laïcité," 23–24.
3. Maira, "Luther révolutionnaire," 101–2.
4. Vovelle, *Révolution française*, 9.
5. Miquel, *Guerres de religion*, 515.

sent to the galleys and prisons. The children of marital unions which had not been blessed by a priest were not considered French. Young girls were still kidnapped and shut up in convents. Pastors were still punished with death. Antoine Court had founded a school for pastoral training in 1730 at Lausanne from which many students would become martyrs. Pastor Durand who preached at Vivarais was hanged in 1732, and Morel-Duvernet was shot to death while attempting to escape from captivity. In 1745 Pastor Roger was hanged at Grenoble; Louis Ranc suffered the same fate the following year. One of the most well-known martyrs was Pastor Rochette, condemned in 1762 and hanged at Toulouse. His crime? He was preparing the baptism of an infant.[6]

Around 1760, a period began called the "Second Desert," to distinguish it from the earlier "Heroic Desert." The French government, consumed with the Seven Years' War (1756–1763), no longer had the means to carry on the occupation of Languedoc where the threat of civil war was always present. The government did not desire a return to war and the Huguenots profited from favorable circumstances to reestablish their churches.[7] At the same time, the illegal situation of Protestants and the persistence of tortures from another age both contributed powerfully to the mobilization of philosophers' opinions against the monarchy. Philosophers, no friends of Huguenots, nonetheless shared the idea of the necessity of separation between the Church and State, and began to defend the Huguenots and decry the barbarity directed toward them. Jean-Jacques Rousseau (1712–1778) published *Du Contrat social ou Principes du droit politique* in 1762 in which he declared that man is born free and everywhere bound in shackles. Voltaire advocated for an enlightened monarchy; Rousseau chose the Republic, but they both condemned the obscurantism of the Church, symbolized by the affairs of Jean Calas, Jean-Paul Sirven, and Jean-François de la Barre.[8] Voltaire led a struggle to restore the name of Calas, tortured and executed after being falsely accused of killing his son to prevent him from converting to Catholicism. He defended Sirven, who in 1762 was accused of killing his daughter who had disappeared and whose body was later found in a well. Only in 1771 was the death sentence quashed and the confiscated possessions of Sirven restored.[9] Voltaire came to the defense of the chevalier de

6. Miquel, *Guerres de religion*, 514.

7. Garrisson, *Histoire des protestants*, 206.

8. Dusseau, "L'histoire de la Séparation," 13.

9. Miquel, *Guerres de religion*, 514.

la Barre, who was condemned to death in 1766 for refusing to remove his hat at the passing of a religious procession. The defense was in vain and the nineteen-year-old chevalier was executed, decapitated, his body burned, and for good measure a banned copy of Voltaire's *Philosophical Dictionary* was added to the flames.[10]

Violence against Protestants gradually subsided and after 1750 the condemnations of believers to the galleys and the executions of pastors became less numerous. The last prisoner entered the Tower of Constance in 1761 and was freed by order of the king one month later. Marie Durand was freed in 1768 after thirty-eight years of confinement. Under pressure, the government finally freed the last detainees in 1769—Suzanne Bouzigue, Suzanne Pagès, and Marie Roue. The pastor Broca, who held assemblies near Meaux, was released from prison; his colleague Charmuzy, who died in prison in 1771 after his arrest and beating, was the last recorded victim of repression.[11] The liberation of the last two survivors of the galleys, Paul Achard and Antoine Riaille, who had been condemned for life in 1745, took place in 1775.[12] By God's grace and providence, the Huguenots survived against all odds in the face of successive, staggering onslaughts of persecution.

EDICT OF TOLERATION

There are different perspectives on the relationship and contribution of Protestantism to the Revolution. It does not appear that Protestants were any more or less revolutionary than other French at the time of the revolution and they were not united on political grounds. With rare exceptions, Reformed believers remained loyal to the monarchy, to Louis XVI as absolute monarch and then as constitutional monarch. Some historians have highlighted the influence of the Reformation on the Revolution and the participation of pastors in the work of revolutionary gatherings, although the actual number of pastors present at these gatherings is difficult to ascertain. Krumenacker asserts that no pastors died for their faith during the Reign of Terror but some were guillotined for their political views. Pastors were also divided on whether to swear a civic oath in 1791. From the available evidence it is difficult to know how Protestants lived and received the

10. Monod, *Sécularisation et laïcité*, 52.

11. Miquel, *Guerres de religion*, 515.

12. Garrisson, *Histoire des protestants*, 215.

events which shook France beginning in 1789. What united Protestants was the desire to obtain equality of rights with other French citizens and the freedom of worship. With the Revolution, Huguenots were finally considered full citizens.[13]

The struggle for freedom of conscience progressed but did not end with the Edict of Toleration, granted by Louis XVI in November 1787, and written for those who did not profess the Catholic religion. The edict provided legal existence and civil status to French Protestants, permitted Protestants to legally marry without a Catholic priest, and their children were considered legitimate. These were individual freedoms but there was not yet unrestricted freedom of worship. That right came later with the Declaration of the Rights of Man and of the Citizen which recognized that all people are born and remain free with equal rights. Yet Louis XVI outlined an implicit recognition of one of the fundamental rights found later in the Declaration. In effect, the king stated that long experience had shown that the rigorous trials imposed on Protestants had been insufficient to convert them to Catholicism and the State must no longer uselessly punish them. The reasoning was pragmatic and an observation of the failure to convert Protestants by force. The text of the edict disappointed many Huguenots. Before the official registration of the edict, the Parliament in Paris made clear that the Catholic religion was the religion of the kingdom with a monopoly on public worship, and Protestants were still denied access to positions in government and education. Still we should not underestimate the importance of this step toward full freedom of religion. It was the dawn of a new era for Protestants.

The tolerance provided by the edict must not be understood in our modern sense. This tolerance was viewed negatively by princes and peoples who were unable to conceptualize tolerance as an "amicable coexistence" of religious communities separated by strong doctrinal differences. Tolerance in a pejorative sense was later transformed from a pragmatic inconvenience to what has been called the *tolérance de Modernes*. This modern tolerance produced rights and new freedoms—freedom of conscience, the free exercise of religion, the freedom of expression and by extension the freedom to blaspheme. The battle for freedom of conscience continued with the involvement of Pastor Rabout Saint-Étienne in the Declaration of the Rights

13. Krumenacker, "Les pasteurs français," 189–94.

of Man and of the Citizen and for the rights of minorities which led to increased religious freedom for Protestants in 1789.[14]

DECLARATION OF THE RIGHTS OF MAN AND OF THE CITIZEN

The Revolution in 1789 introduced sweeping changes in France. Religious liberty was proclaimed and activities transferred from the Church to the State (i.e., civil status, marriage). The State introduced legal divorce, abolished religious crimes of blasphemy, heresy, and sorcery, and adopted a revolutionary calendar.[15] Article 10 of the 1789 *Déclaration des droits de l'homme et du citoyen* recognized the liberty of opinion and declared that no one should be disturbed for their opinions, not even religious ones, as long as their expression did not disturb the public order (*Nul ne doit être inquiété pour ses opinions, même religieuses, pourvu que leur manifestation ne trouble pas l'ordre public établi par la Loi*). Protestants largely welcomed with favor the Revolution which brought about their emancipation from the intolerance and persecution at the hands of the Catholic Church.[16] They had received limited civil status rights in 1787. In 1789 they were granted equal rights and the freedom of worship. The Assembly tacitly authorized them to organize at their discretion, which they did notably in opening places of worship in cities where that had been previously forbidden.[17] They attached themselves to the principles of 1789 and to the Revolution and enjoyed the protection of the government until the Terror of 1793 of which they condemned the excesses.[18] Even during the Terror, when many temples, churches, and synagogues were closed and public worship was forbidden, Protestants did not lose the freedom of conscience or the freedom of private worship. For this reason the memories of the Terror quickly faded.[19] Many Reformed pastors and believers, however, seduced by patriotism or natural religion, readily accepted the worship of the Supreme Being, saw in it the cessation of confessional rivalries, and the end of the sentiment of being part of a sect. Reformed churches struggled to rebuild

14. Lacorne, *Les frontières*, 11–12.
15. CNEF, *Laïcité française*, 13.
16. Vovelle, *Révolution française*, 22.
17. De Montclos, *Histoire religieuse*, 106.
18. Boyer, *La loi de 1905*, 69.
19. Encrevé, "Les huguenots du XIXe siècle," 549.

spiritually, many characterized by spiritual lukewarmness. The number of pastors decreased and intellectual life was marked by eighteenth-century rationalism. In Garrisson's opinion, the Revolution, in spite of appearances, ultimately was not beneficial for Reformed churches. Yet the realization of the freedom of religion would permit future progress.[20]

The execution of Louis XVI for treason on January 21,1793 prepared the way for further changes in the Church-State relationship. Two groups, *la Gironde* and *la Montagne*, disputed his fate. The former group, a political entity formed in 1791 by several deputies from the region by the same name, argued for clemency.[21] The latter group, among whom was Robespierre, referred to elevated places at the Convention where the political left sat led by Robespierre and Danton.[22] According to Robespierre, the Revolution required virtue and terror, "virtue, without which terror is harmful; and terror, without which virtue is powerless. Terror is nothing other than prompt, severe, inflexible justice. It is an emanation of virtue."[23] In 1795, the separation of Church and State was introduced constitutionally for the first time. The arrival of Napoleon would throw these separatist initiatives into confusion when he seized the initiative to bring religion into his service. Yet the future would reveal that many people freed from obligatory religious duties and rituals would soon fall away from an organized religion which no longer wielded political power. Over the next one hundred years the work of the Revolution was constantly threatened with the successive rise and fall of republics and empires.

The Revolution would not remain unopposed by the Catholic Church. The battle for republican values intensified while the Church fought vigorously to reverse the losses suffered under the Revolution. The Church had its defenders and the Counter-Revolution continued the battle for ideas and divided France into two camps reminiscent of the Wars of Religion. The counter-revolutionaries, many of whom had lost privileges, whose lands were confiscated and titles revoked, sought the restoration of the monarchy. The Revolution was interrupted with the coup d'état and rise to power of Napoleon Bonaparte in 1799 followed by his ascension as hereditary emperor in 1804. After his exile and death, the ideals of the Revolution would return in force and compete with counter-revolutionary forces for

20. Garrisson, *Histoire des protestants*, 235–37.

21. *Nouveau Petit Robert*, 1154.

22. *Nouveau Petit Robert*, 1630.

23. Robespierre, *Œuvres*, 357.

the next century. Over the next one hundred years the work of the Revolution was constantly threatened with the successive rise and fall of republics and empires. There was not, however, any turning back the clock. Surely, the struggles would continue. Yet after three centuries of epic resistance and unimaginable suffering, the Huguenots finally achieved the longing of their hearts—freedom of conscience and freedom to worship their God!

Although the nineteenth century was not without religious conflict, the Concordat, signed in 1801 between Napoleon and Pope Pius VII, effectively put an end to systematic religious persecution and civil war. The Concordat recognized that Catholicism was not the religion of the State but the majority religion of French citizens. Three confessions—Lutheran, Reformed, and later Jewish—were recognized alongside the Catholic Church with legal status and overt persecution of Protestants ceased.[24] The Concordat signaled an end to three intense centuries of violence in the struggle for religious freedom. In another sense, however, the struggle never ended. Almost a hundred years of relative peace followed the Concordat until events at end of the nineteenth century led to the unraveling of the Concordat and the enactment of the Law of Separation of Churches and State in 1905.[25] It was always and only a relative peace because there were still attempts in the nineteenth century to undermine the gains of the Revolution and reestablish the monarchy.[26] Indeed, under Louis XVIII (1755–1824) and the Restoration in 1814 Catholicism was reaffirmed as the religion of the State, tensions grew at times between Catholics and Protestants, and ancient antagonisms were revived. Protestants were less numerous in France after centuries of persecution and with hundreds of thousands settled in countries of refuge. There was an estimated seven hundred fifty thousand Protestants for thirty-five million Catholics in France in 1850. Apart from Alsace, Protestants had sizeable communities only in regions with difficult access like the mountains of the Drôme, the Ardèche, or the Cévennes, and continued to experience discrimination. The great majority of Huguenots were peasants living in rural areas and the upper class Protestants, often known as *Haute Société Protestant* or H.S.P., represented a small minority.[27]

---

24. Machelon, *La laïcité demain*, 17.

25. See the author's book, *Rise of French Laïcité: French Secularism from the Reformation to the Twenty-first Century* (Pickwick, 2020), for a discussion of the events leading to the disestablishment of the Catholic Church in France.

26. Cabanel, "La question religieuse," 171.

27. Encrevé, "Les huguenots du XIXe siècle," 547–48.

Freedom of conscience and worship, state support for pastors' salaries, liberal influences, and the attribution of places of worship all led to new challenges for Protestantism in succeeding centuries. That story is still being told. We end here, however, with the Revolution and Concordat although the history of the Huguenots continues to our day in the faithful witness of French Reformed churches, in places where they found refuge, and through organizations which exist to perpetuate their memory.

Conclusion

THIS SURVEY OF THREE hundred years of Huguenot resistance reveals the remarkable impact of the Reformation in France which set in motion the unstoppable aspirations of people for the freedom of conscience and the freedom to worship God without state or religious coercion. We have seen that in the early years of the sixteenth century, humanism opened the door for the study of biblical texts and led to an evangelical movement throughout Europe. Many, like Erasmus and Lefèvre d'Étaples, sought reform of the Church from within. François I's reaction against protests and the disruption of religious unity was to maintain the Church's authority. Beginning in 1516 with the Concordat of Bologna, François I enhanced his power and became the champion of the French Catholic Church which had long sought her independence from the Roman Curia with the help of the monarchy.[1] The French monarchy claimed the title *très chrétien* and married Catholicism and loyalty to the State. From 1534 to 1559 Protestantism spread rapidly in spite of persecution. The Church pursued a strategy to stamp out heresy and counterattacked with the Council of Trent (1545–1563). Henri II followed the repressive tactics of François I to halt the spread of Protestantism and brought economic ruin and deeper divisions in the kingdom. Much of the nobility was either won over to the Reformation or ruffled by the strengthening of an absolute monarchy. Prior to the Wars of Religion, Protestants numbered around two million, or ten percent of the population in 1560, with many more sympathetic to the new religion, and their numbers were reduced year after year to a small minority.[2]

After the short reign of François II, under whom the house of Guise grew in influence, and after the vain and hypocritical attempts of Catherine

1. Garrisson, *Histoire des protestants*, 20.

2. Garrisson, *Histoire des protestants*, 54.

de Médicis for conciliation, the Wars of Religion broke out for over thirty years. Peace was elusive because of fanaticism on both sides and broken treaties. The Huguenot numbers were reduced by war and by massacres, by exile, or by a return to Catholicism. The abjuration of Henri IV (1593) and the Edict of Nantes (1598) brought peace to the kingdom under a Catholic dynasty with the intention to establish religious unity.[3] Boldly, the king labored to have the two religions live together only to have his dream shattered when assassinated in 1610. His successors, born in Catholicism and committed to stamp out heresy, conspired to return France to religious unity, or better, to a religious monopoly. Under Louis XIII, the Protestants lost their places of security, and under Louis XIV persecution increased. The royal government pursued by any means the mass conversion of dissidents. Finally, in 1685, Louis XIV revoked the Edict of Nantes, but the Revocation failed to wipe out French Protestantism. The War of the Camisards manifested the indomitable fortitude of the Huguenots of the Midi. The Protestant minority, whether enslaved on the king's ships, imprisoned, or gathering secretly in the "Desert," waited with a rare constancy for better days that the Edict of Toleration (1787) and the Revolution (1789) would finally bring.[4]

For three hundred years, the Huguenots were decimated by war, deceived by edicts of pacification, forced to convert, banished from their homeland, and betrayed by their neighbors; they were not destroyed. Their numbers today might appear negligible, their influence imperceptible, and their beliefs misunderstood and caricatured. Yet, after centuries of suffering, of massacres, of hatred and repressions, deprived of legal rights, they endured and remain today as a testimony to their enduring faith and the grace of God. The great emancipating project for the freedom of conscience and the freedom of expression, inaugurated in the sixteenth century and generalized in the following centuries, continues to be fought in France. The very conceptions of tolerance have evolved from one century to another up until now, but their final object remains the same: tolerance leads to religious pluralism, whatever may be the nature of relations between Churches and the State.[5] The struggle in France for these freedoms would eventually lead to the "*Loi du 9 décembre 1905 concernant la séparation des Églises et de l'État*" which finally enshrined legally the right of freedom of

3. Stéphan, *L'Épopée huguenote*, 277–79.

4. Stéphan, *L'Épopée huguenote*, 276–77.

5. Lacorne, *Les frontières*, 9.

conscience. The arrival of the law of 1905 ended centuries of harsh combats between religious and secular powers.[6]

In the twentieth-first century, unbelief with its own creeds, myths, and shibboleths has won the day in many places as the dominant religion. In the past, unbelievers and dissenters were persecuted for their lack of conformity to the prevailing powers. In our day it is much more likely that unbelief and a godless political agenda exercise state repression against those who hold opposing views, who are stigmatized for their beliefs, and marginalized from society. These are often believers who dissent from an all-tolerant enlightened progressivism which cannot tolerate those who hold to traditional beliefs concerning marriage, family, the unborn, and gender, to name a few. Religious convictions and dissenting voices are not merely offensive but now are considered "hate speech" in order to criminalize religious belief. The emergence of the presence of Islam at a time of disenchantment with European secularization has generated tensions in all of Europe, and the growth of evangelicalism, often viewed as a foreign cult, has raised questions about its place in the Republic.[7]

After years of terrorist acts and the growing influence in France of radical Islam, the French government has decided to act, and rightly so, since one of the functions of the State is to assure the security of its citizens. Religions and religious choices are protected by the State as long as they do not contravene constitutional values and disturb the public order. It is normal that France takes steps to preserve a measure of peaceful coexistence in society. In many countries from which Muslims have entered France, the two dimensions of religion and politics are mingled. The struggle between competing visions of Islam in non-Islamic nations such as France continues to unfold as Muslims either adapt to secular society or resist integration and embrace communitarianism. Radical Islam (Islamism) considers Europe immoral, a Europe which no longer inspires respect or the desire of Muslims to assimilate.[8] Radical Islam contests the established principles of the separation of Church and State. With demographic changes in France and with Islam the second largest religion in France, there is growing visibility of Islam in public space. The problem is not the long presence of Muslims in France, but the radicalization of Islam in the 1990s. The issues now include employees in the public sector who are obligated to be neutral

6. Soppelsa, "De la laïcité," 2.

7. Baubérot, Les laïcités dans le monde, 106.

8. Chauprade, "Islam et islamisme," 100.

in religious matters, hospitals where Muslim women refuse to be treated by male doctors, and school debate on displaying religious symbols in dress and accessories.[9] These changes in French society have resulted in enormous pressure to halt the advance of religious inroads in France which are in contradiction to the ideals of liberty, equality, and fraternity which date to the French Revolution.

For centuries in France, the State has been one of the major actors in the process of the removal of religion from the public sphere. Although this has happened elsewhere, in France there has been a greater marginalization of religion.[10] The separate spheres of Church and State are now threatened since religions have emerged from the private sphere and have become a problem for society and for political authorities. The religious landscape has changed in France with the presence of Islam and the advances of Protestant evangelicalism.[11] The freedoms of conscience and worship are considered by many as only individual rights which must not undermine republican values.[12] Religions, however, should not sit under the judgment of the State for their teaching or way of life. They are defined and judged, not by their beliefs, but by any actions which are criminal in nature.[13] So it is normal that questions are being asked as new religious issues arise in a multi-confessional, pluralistic society and whether there are forms of religious community which are not acceptable in a democratic society or subvert the social order.[14] Our survey of Huguenot history has demonstrated that heresy was a crime punishable by the State. Only time will tell how far the State will go in criminalizing evangelical beliefs and speech that run counter to the prevailing relativistic ethos, and condemn values that are contrary to the redefinition of many long-established traditional beliefs. Most evangelical believers are willing to express genuine tolerance in a pluralistic society and do not seek to impose their beliefs and practices on others. They cannot, however, affirm or validate beliefs and practices that are contrary to their convictions.

One of the pressing questions relating to Islam and its place in French society concerns Islam's compatibility with the values of the French

9. Dusseau, "L'histoire de la Séparation," 22.

10. Gauchet, *La religion dans la démocratie*, 41.

11. Williame, "L'expression des religions," 5–6.

12. Coq, *Laïcité et République*, 257–58.

13. Pena-Ruiz, *Qu'est-ce que la laïcité?*, 94–95.

14. Coq, *Laïcité et République*, 255.

Republic. Over the past five years there have been at least twenty-five terrorist attacks in France with hundreds of victims. On July 14, 2016, a truck entered the Promenade des Anglais in Nice and ran over people who were there to watch fireworks. Eighty-four people died and over four hundred were wounded. More recently in October 2020, a schoolteacher, Samuel Paty, was decapitated by radical Islamists after being accused of denigrating Islam. Multiple arrests followed. These tragic events have become all too common in France. These incidents have also shaped divergent views on the capacity of Islam to adapt to Western society.[15] The perpetrators are clearly identifiable; they are not followers of evangelical Christianity nor do they represent the majority of Muslims. They are radical jihadists hostile to democracy. At the time of writing this book, the French government was debating and preparing to vote on a law purportedly to safeguard republican values (Law to Uphold Republican Principles). First presented in December 2020, an initial version of the bill was passed by the National Assembly in February 2021.[16] The opening text declares that the Republic rests on the pillars of *la liberté, l'égalité, la fraternité, l'éducation,* and *la laïcité* and recognizes that the insidious gangrene eroding France's values is essentially Islamist. France's response to radical Islam sadly includes evangelical Christians as part of the problem of *séparatisme* in order to not give the impression of targeting Islam and to avoid charges of religious discrimination. The law's proposals, under intense discussion and scrutiny, appear to have opened a breach in the 1905 Law of Separation regarding government neutrality in religious matters. Never mind that evangelical Christians, now under suspicion, who represent about 1 percent of the French population, support the concerns of the government to provide security for its citizens. On February 2, 2021, Gérald Darmanin, Minister of the Interior, affirmed that there can be no discussion with people who refuse to recognize that the law of the Republic is superior to the law of God. The next day Darmanin went further in targeting evangelicals as an important problem and denounced their supposed foreign financing. Sébastien Fath recognizes that there is the possibility of a small number of evangelicals who have sectarian tendencies, yet without any incitation to violence. The proposed project of law unfairly scapegoats evangelicals who support the Republic and her laws.[17] The historian Mabry observed that because we disdain history by

15. Zeghal, "La constitution," 1–2.

16. https://www.assemblee-nationale.fr/dyn/15/textes/l15b3649_projet-loi.

17. See *Le Figaro*, February 5, 2021, "Non, les évangéliques ne représentent pas un

ignorance, by laziness, or by the presumption to profit from the experience of past centuries, each century brings back the spectacle of the same errors and the same calamities.[18] Freedoms acquired over the last centuries are under attack today in France. This situation finds parallels in Huguenot history. The Huguenots professed loyalty to the Crown and yet were identified as enemies of the State and objects of increased suspicion and surveillance.

The CNEF (Conseil national des évangéliques de France), which represents seven hundred thousand evangelicals in France, more than 70 percent of Protestant churches, two thousand five hundred places of worship, and one hundred sixty associations, has been at the forefront of attempts to introduce balance in the government's ambitions to address religious radicalism. In May 2021 they submitted a request to the UN Human Rights Commission to examine France's respect of religious freedom, the impact of proposed modifications to the 1905 Law of Separation of Churches and State, new constraints and obligations placed on churches, and limits on religious freedom in public space.[19] The new law, under discussion by a joint committee of deputies and senators, is scheduled for a vote in July 2021. Evangelicals have cause for concern since the law proposes increased surveillance and new constraints for churches. Among the concerns are the government's interference in the finances of churches, mandatory reporting to the government of funds received, and authorization not only for homeschooling children but authorization for the subject matter taught. In addition, the proposed law prohibits minors and parents accompanying children on school outings from wearing religious symbols in public.[20] The future, therefore, does not appear serene for evangelicals as they continue to be the object of unjust attacks by government officials either through ignorance or maliciousness. The form of government control and intrusion into religion has changed. We are reminded of the need for vigilance and prayer. If history teaches us anything, we should know that the struggle of the Huguenots in their resistance to government interference in spiritual matters continues in our day.

'problème très important' en France." https://www.lefigaro.fr/vox/societe/non-les-evangeliques-ne-representent-pas-un-probleme-tres-important-en-france-20210205.

18. Mably, "L'histoire doit être une école," 264.

19. https://tbinternet.ohchr.org/Treaties/CCPR/Shared%20Documents/FRA/INT_CCPR_ICS_FRA_44848_F.pdf.

20. See "Projet de loi pour renforcer les principes républicains: loi de surveillance?" https://www.lecnef.org/articles/73961-pjl-principes-republicains-une-loi-de-surveillance.

The portrayal of Old Testament martyrs found in the Epistle to the Hebrews fittingly describes the Huguenots in their victories and their defeats.

> Hebrews 11: 32 And what more shall I say? For time would fail me to tell of Gideon, Barak, Samson, Jephthah, of David and Samuel and the prophets— 33 who through faith conquered kingdoms, enforced justice, obtained promises, stopped the mouths of lions, 34 quenched the power of fire, escaped the edge of the sword, were made strong out of weakness, became mighty in war, put foreign armies to flight. 35 Women received back their dead by resurrection. Some were tortured, refusing to accept release, so that they might rise again to a better life. 36 Others suffered mocking and flogging, and even chains and imprisonment. 37 They were stoned, they were sawn in two, they were killed with the sword. They went about in skins of sheep and goats, destitute, afflicted, mistreated— 38 of whom the world was not worthy—wandering about in deserts and mountains, and in dens and caves of the earth.

Of whom the world was not worthy and who departed from this world as enemies of the State and of the Church which hounded and executed them. We understand then why Protestants, who had suffered decades of intolerance and violence, whose loved ones groaned in dungeons or died miserably on the king's galleys, and whose lands were invaded and devasted by the king's troops and foreign invaders, at times took up arms to obtain their God-given religious rights which had been taken away from them by force.

The story of the Huguenots is still not widely known. Let us hear it once again and weep, and rejoice, and resist with prayer and perseverance! Whatever befalls the people of God in any age does not remove the sure hope in the promises of God. May the church of Jesus Christ in France remain vigilant and faithful to the Savior. May the gospel shine forth in power in transforming lives for the glory of God and the good of the nation. Believers may not die a martyr's death as did many Huguenots, but if they do, may they die with the unfailing courage, unshakeable faith, and enduring confidence of the Huguenots. Jesus will surely keep the promise made to his true Church: "Be faithful unto death, and I will give you the crown of life" (Rev 2:10).

Chronology

1547	Henri II establishes *chambre ardente* to destroy the spread of Protestantism
1553	Five students burned alive at Lyon
1555	First Reformed churches in France; Peace of Augsburg
1557	Battle of Saint-Quentin
1558	Death of Emperor Charles V
1559	Death of Henri II in jousting accident
1559–1560	Reign of François II
1559	National synod in Paris and Reformed confession of faith; Execution of parliamentarian Anne du Bourg; Edict of Écouen; Treaty of Cateau-Cambrésis
1560	Conspiracy of Amboise to kidnap François II; Estates General in Orléans
1560–1574	Reign of Charles IX; Catherine de Médicis regent
1561	Colloquium of Poissy and Theodore Beza; Jeanne d'Albret, queen of Navarre, acclaimed by Protestants in Paris
1562	Edict of January by Catherine de Médicis; Massacre of Protestants at Vassy in Champagne begins first war of religion; Treaty of Hampton-Court between Huguenots and Queen Elizabeth I
1563	Edict of Amboise ends first war of religion
1564	Death of Calvin; Treaty of Troyes
1567	Second war of religion begins
1568	Edict of Longjumeau ends second war of religion and reestablishes the Edict of Amboise; Third war of religion begins in September; Edict of Saint-Maur prohibits all religions except Catholicism
1569	Battles of Jarnac and Moncontour; Condé killed
1570	Edict of Saint-Germain ends third war of religion
1571	La Rochelle Confession of Faith
1572	Marriage of Henri de Navarre and Marguerite de Valois (Aug 18); Gaspard de Coligny wounded in assassination attempt (Aug 22); Coligny assassinated and Saint Bartholomew's Day massacre in Paris (Aug 24); Fourth war of religion begins
1573	Siege of La Rochelle; Edict of La Rochelle ends fourth war of religion
1574–1589	Reign of Henri III
1574	Fifth war of religion begins

1576	Henri de Navarre escapes from court in February; Peace of Monsieur (Edict of Beaulieu) ends fifth war of religion; Formation of Catholic League; Estates General in Blois
1577	Sixth war of religion from March to September ends with Peace of Bergerac; Edict of Poitiers
1579	Treaty of Nérac
1579–1580	Short-lived seventh war of religion ends with Treaty of Fleix
1584	Death of François d'Alençon, Duke of Anjou; Henri de Navarre becomes heir to the throne
1585	Edict of Nemours renounces all previous edicts of pacification; Henri de Navarre excommunicated by Pope Sixtus V
1587	Battle of Coutras, major victory for Henri de Navarre
1588	Day of the Barricades; Henri III takes refuge at Chartres; Edict of Union; assassinations of Henri de Guise and cardinal of Guise
1589	Death of Catherine de Médicis; Assassination of Henri III; Charles X crowned by Guises
1589–1610	Reign of Henri IV (crowned in 1594)
1590	Siege of Paris by the army of Henri IV
1591	Edict of Mantes revokes Henri III's edicts
1592	Siege of Rouen by the army of Henri IV
1593	Henri IV abjures Protestantism
1594	Coronation of Henri IV at Chartres
1595	Henri IV receives papal absolution from Pope Clement VIII; Henri IV declares war against Spain
1598	Edict of Nantes ends eighth war of religion; Henri IV signs peace treaty with Philip II of Spain (Peace of Vervins)
1600	Marriage of Henri IV to Marie de Médicis
1603	Henri IV recalls Jesuits from exile
1610	Assassination of Henri IV; Government of Louis XIII led by Marie de Médicis
1610–1643	Reign of Louis XIII
1616	Treaty of Loudun
1617	Concini assassinated
1620	Catholic worship reestablished at Béarn
1621	Military campaign against the Huguenots in the Midi
1622	Peace of Montpellier
1624	Cardinal Richelieu admitted to royal court

1626	Peace of Paris (Treaty of La Rochelle) with R.P.R (*religion prétendue réformée*)
1628	Fall of La Rochelle
1629	Edict of Grace (Peace of Alès) ends civil war
1635	France enters Thirty Years' War
1638	Louis XIII consecrates France to the Virgin
1642	Death of Cardinal Richelieu
1643	Death of Louis XIII
1643–1715	Reign of Louis XIV
1643–1661	Cardinal Mazarin at court
1648	Peace of Westphalia ends the Thirty Years' War
1652	Promise of maintenance of Edict of Nantes
1656	*Commissions* appointed to judge infringements of the Edict of Nantes
1676	Funds provided for conversions (*caisse de conversion*)
1681	*Dragonnades* unleashed to force Protestant conversions
1682	Louis XIV moves court to Versailles
1685	Revocation of the Edict of Nantes (Edict of Fontainebleau)
1689	Return of Claude Brousson and François Vivent to the Cévennes
1692	Vivent killed defending himself from capture
1698	Brousson executed at Montpellier
1700s	Church of the Desert; prophetism in the Cévennes and Bas-Languedoc
1702	Murder of the abbot of Chaila; Execution of Esprit Séguier
1702–1705	War of the Camisards
1704	Departure of Cavalier; Death of Rolland
1705	Execution of Castanet
1710	Death of Abraham Mazel
1715	Death of Louis XIV; Antoine Court and first synod of the Desert
1724	Louis XV reinstitutes Edict of Revocation and repression against Huguenots
1730	Marie Durand imprisoned in Tower of Constance
1762	Last pastor executed and last condemnation to the galleys
1768	Marie Durand released from Tower of Constance (died in 1776)
1771	François Charmuzy, last recorded victim of repression

CHRONOLOGY

1775	Last galley prisoners released
1787	Edict of Toleration
1789	French Revolution and Declaration of the Rights of Man and of the Citizen
1793	Reign of Terror; Louis XVI executed
1801	Concordat of Napoleon with Rome (in effect until 1905)

Bibliography

Armogathe, Jean-Robert, and Philippe Joutard. "Bâville et la guerre des camisards." *Revue d'histoire moderne et contemporaine* 19 (January–March 1972) 45–72. https://www.persee.fr/doc/rhmc_0048-8003_1972_num_19_1_2183.

Augeron, Mickaël, et al. *La Rochelle: Capitale atlantique, capitale huguenote.* Paris: Éditions du Patrimoine, 1998.

Bainton, Roland H. *The Reformation of the Sixteenth Century.* Boston: Beacon Press, 1952.

Bastide, Samuel. *Les prisonnières de la Tour de Constance.* Mialet, France: Musée du Désert, 1901.

Baubérot, Jean. *Les laïcités dans le monde.* 4th ed. Paris: Presses universitaires de France, 2016.

Baubérot, Jean and Marianne Carbonnier-Burkard. *Histoire des Protestants: Une minorité en France (XVIe–XXIe siècle).* Paris: Éditions Ellipses, 2016.

Benedict, Philip. "The Wars of Religion, 1562–1598." In *Renaissance and Reformation France, 1500-1648,* edited by Mack P. Holt, 147–75. New York: Oxford University Press, 2002.

Benedict, Philip and Virginia Reinburg. "Religion and the Sacred." In *Renaissance and Reformation France,* 1500–1648, edited by Mack P. Holt, 119–46. New York: Oxford University Press, 2002.

Benoist, Élie. *Histoire de l'édit de Nantes.* Delft: Adrian Beman, 1690. https://gallica.bnf.fr/ark:/12148/bpt6k9601611f.texteImage.

Benoit, Daniel. *Marie Durand, prisonnière à la Tour de Constance de 1730 à 1768: Son temps, sa famille, ses compagnes de captivité.* Seraing, Belgium: Edipro, 2008.

Birnstiel, Eckart. "La conversion des protestants sous le régime de l'Édit de Nantes (1598–1685)." In *Religions, pouvoir et violence,* edited by Patrick Cabanel and Michel Bertrand, 93–113. Toulouse: Presses universitaires du Midi, 2004.

Bloch, Jonathan. *La Réforme Protestante, de Luther à Calvin: La réponse aux abus de la religion catholique.* Namur, Belgium: Lemaitre, 2015.

Blough, Neil. "La persécution intra-chrétienne au seizième siècle." *Théologie évangélique* 18 (2019) 5–16.

Bost, Charles. *Histoire des Protestants de France.* 9th ed. Carrières-sous-Poissy, France: Éditions La Cause, 1996.

———. *Les martyrs d'Aigues-Mortes.* Nîmes: C. Lacour, 1997.

———. *Les prédicants protestants des Cévennes et du Bas-Languedoc, 1684–1700.* Paris: Librairie ancienne Honoré. Champion, 1912.

Bourgeon, Jean-Louis. *L'assassinat de Coligny.* Geneva: Librairie Droz, 1992.

Boyer, Alain. *La loi de 1905: hier, aujourd'hui, demain.* Lyon: Éditions Olivetan, 2005.

Bray, Gerald. "Late-Medieval Theology." In *Reformation Theology,* edited by Michael Barrett, 67–110. Wheaton, IL: Crossway, 2017.

Bruley, Yves, ed. *1905, la séparation des Églises et de l'État: Les textes fondateurs.* Paris: Éditions Perrin, 2004.

Buisseret, David. *Henry IV.* Boston: George Allen & Unwin, 1984.

Cabanel, Patrick. "Au miroir du Pluralisme: Minorités Protestantes et Juives en Europe du XVIe au XXe siècle." *Revue d'histoire du protestantisme* 2 (October–December 2017) 485–504. https://www.jstor.org/stable/44850999.

———. "Enchanter, désenchanter l'histoire du Refuge huguenot." *Revue d'histoire du protestantisme* 2 (July–September 2017) 409–20. https://www.jstor.org/stable/4485 0967.

———. *Histoire des protestants en France.* Paris: Fayard, 2012.

———. "La 'question religieuse' et les solutions en France (XVI–XXI siècle)." In *La Laïcité, une question au présent,* edited by Jean Birnbaum et al., 165–84. Nantes: Éditions Cécile Defaut, 2006.

Cabanel, Patrick, and Michel Bertrand, ed. *Religions, pouvoir et violence.* Toulouse: Presses universitaires du Midi, 2004.

Calvin, Jean. *Lettres de Jean Calvin, recueillies pour la première fois et publiées d'après les manuscrits originaux.* Paris: Meyrueis and Compagne, 1854.

———. *L'Institution chrétienne.* Chicago: Éditions Kerygma, Éditions Farel, 1978. Reprint of 1955–58 edition.

Cameron, Euan. *The European Reformation.* 2nd ed. Oxford: Oxford University Press, 1991.

Carbonnier-Burkard, Marianne. *La révolte des Camisards.* Rennes: Éditions Ouest-France, 2012.

Carenco, Jean-François. *L'Édit de Nantes: Sûreté et Education,* edited by Marie-José Lacava and Robert Guicharnaud. Montauban: Société Montalbanaise d'Étude et de Recherche sur le Protestantisme, 1999.

Chamson, André. *Suite Camisarde.* Paris: Éditions Omnibus, 2002.

Chaunu, Pierre. *Le temps des Réformes: Histoire religieuse et système de civilisation. La crise de la chrétienté., L'éclatement (1250–1550).* Paris: Fayard, 1997.

Chauprade, Aymeric. "Islam et islamisme." *Revue Politique et Parlementaire* 1038 (January–March 2006) 95–101.

Christin, Olivier. *Les Réformes: Luther, Calvin et les protestants.* Paris: Découvertes Gallimard, 1995.

CNEF. *Laïcité française: Entre l'idée, l'Histoire, et le droit positif.* In Les Textes du CNEF. Marpent, France: Éditions BLF, 2013.

Coq, Guy. *Laïcité et République: Le lien nécessaire.* Paris: Éditions du Félin, 2003.

Cottret, Bernard. *1598, L'Édit de Nantes: Pour en finir avec les guerres de religion.* Paris: Perrin, 1997.

———. *Histoire de la Réforme protestante.* Paris: Perrin, 2010.

Coudy, Julien. *The Huguenot Wars: An Eyewitness Account.* Translated by Julie Kernan. Philadelphia: Chilton, 1969.

Crété, Liliane. *Coligny.* Paris: Fayard, 1985.

Crouzet, Denis. *La genèse de la Réforme française (1520–1562).* Paris: Sedes, 1996.

Daireaux, Luc. *Réduire les Huguenots: Protestants et pouvoirs en Normandie au XVIIe siècle.* Paris: Honoré Champion, 2010.

————. "Louis XIV et les protestants normands: Autour de la révocation de l'édit de Nantes." *Bulletin de la Société de l'Histoire du Protestantisme Français* (1903–2015) 158 (January–March 2012) 123–32. https://www.jstor.org/stable/24310203.

Danclos, Anne. *Marie Durand et les captives d'Aigues-Mortes*. Nîmes: C. Lacour, 1993.

Daussy, Hugues. *Les huguenots et le roi: Le combat politique de Philippe Duplessis-Mornay (1572–1600)*. Geneva: Droz, 2002.

————. "Les huguenots entre l'obéissance au roi et l'obéissance à Dieu." *Nouvelle Revue du Seizième Siècle* 22 (2004) 49–69. https://www.jstor.org/stable/25599002.

Davis, Stephen M. *Rise of French Laïcité: French Secularism from the Reformation to the Twenty-first Century*. Eugene, OR: Pickwick, 2020.

Delteil, Jacques. "Allocutions au Musée du Désert: Un Cévenol qui refuse l'exclusion: François Vivent." *Bulletin de la Société de l'Histoire du Protestantisme Français* (1903–2015) 139 (January–March 1993) 127–32. http://www.jstor.org/stable/24297159.

Delumeau, Jean. *Le christianisme va-t-il mourir?* Paris: Hachette Édition, 1977.

Delumeau, Jean, Thierry Wanegffelen, and Bernard Cottret. *Naissance et affirmation de la Réforme*. Presses universitaires de France, 2012.

De Montclos, Xavier. *Histoire religieuse de la France*. Paris: Presses universitaires de France, 1988.

De Waele, Michel. "Le cadavre du conspirateur: Peur, colère et défense de la communauté à l'époque de la Saint-Barthélemy." *Revue d'histoire moderne et contemporaine* 64 (January–March 2017) 97–115. http://www.jstor.org/stable/44986654.

Diefendorf, Barbara B. *Beneath the Cross: Catholics and Huguenots in Sixteenth-Century Paris*. New York: Oxford University Press, 1991.

Dixon, C. Scott. "Martin Luther and the Reformation in Historical Thought, 1517–2017." *Studies: An Irish Quarterly Review* 106 (2017) 404–16.

Dousset, Christine. "Entre tolérance et violence: La Révolution française et la question religieuse." In *Religions, pouvoir et violence*, edited by Patrick Cabanel and Michel Bertrand, 114–25. Toulouse: Presses universitaires du Midi, 2004.

Doumergue, Émile. *Le vrai chant du vrai psaume huguenot*. Valence-sur-Rhône, France: Imprimeries Réunies, 1929.

Dusseau, Joëlle. "L'histoire de la Séparation: Entre permanences et ruptures." *Revue Politique et Parlementaire* 1038 (January–March 2006) 13–22.

Elton, G. R. *Reformation Europe: 1517–1559*. 2nd ed. Malden, MA: Blackwell, 1999.

Encrevé, André. "Les huguenots du XIXe siècle." *Bulletin de la Société de l'Histoire du Protestantisme Français* (1903–2015) 142 (October–December 1996) 547–85. https://www.jstor.org/stable/43498889.

————. *Les protestants et la vie politique française: De la Révolution à nos jours*. Paris: CRNS Éditions, 2020.

Engammare, Max. "Calvin monarchomaque? Du soupçon à l'argument." *Archiv für Reformationsgeschichte* 89 (1998). 207–26. https://doi.org/10.14315/arg-1998-jg14.

Exbrayat, Idebert. *Calvisson, ville Huguenot (1501–1914)*. Nîmes: Librairie Lacour, 1985.

Fabre, André. *Marie Durand, prisonnière de la Tour de Constance, 1712–1768*. Dieulefit, France: Nouvelle société d'éditions de Toulouse, 1935.

Foa, Jérémie. "Les droits fragiles: L'insécurité juridique des huguenots au temps des guerres de Religion." *Revue d'histoire moderne et contemporaine* 64 (April–June 2017) 93–108. https://www.jstor.org/stable/26905641.

Gaillard, Jean-Michel. "L'invention de la laïcité (1598–1905)." In 1905, *la séparation des Églises et de l'État: Les textes fondateurs*, edited by Yves Bruley, 19–36. Paris: Éditions Perrin, 2004.

Gamonnet, Étienne. *Lettres de Marie Durand*. Montpellier: Presses du Languedoc, 1986.

Garrioch, David. *The Huguenots of Paris and the Coming of Religious Freedom, 1685–1789*. Cambridge: Cambridge University Press, 2014.

Garrisson, Janine. *Henri IV*. Paris: Le Seuil, 2008.

———. ed. *Histoire des protestants en France: De la Réforme a la Révolution*. 2nd ed. Toulouse: Éditions Privat, 2001.

———. *L'édit de Nantes: Chronique d'une paix attendue*. Paris: Fayard, 1998.

———. *L'édit de Nantes et sa révocation: Histoire d'une intolérance*. Paris: Le Seuil, 1985.

———. *Les protestants au XVIe siècle*. Paris: Fayard, 1997.

Gauchet, Marcel. *La religion dans la démocratie: Parcours de la laïcité*. Paris: Éditions Gallimard, 1998.

Giraudier, Fanny. "La rébellion du duc de Bouillon: De la querelle nobiliaire à l'affaire d'État (1602–1606)." *Revue d'histoire du protestantisme* 2 (July–September 2017) 339–56. https://www.jstor.org/stable/44850964.

Gray, Janet Glenn. *The French Huguenots: Anatomy of Courage*. Grand Rapids: Baker, 1981.

Harai, Dénes. *Au nom de la reine: Henri de Navarre, lieutenant général de Jeanne d'Albret (1572)*. Pau: Presses universitaires de Pau et des Pays de l'Adour, 2019.

Holt, Mack P. *The French Wars of Religion, 1562–1629*. Cambridge: Cambridge University Press, 1995.

———. "The Kingdom of France in the sixteenth century." In *Renaissance and Reformation France, 1500–1648*. In Short Oxford History of France, edited by William Doyle, 5–26. New York: Oxford University Press, 2002.

Jalla, Jean. *Histoire des Vaudois des Alpes et de leurs colonies*. Pignerol: Imprimerie Sociale, 1922.

Janzé, Charles Alfred. *Les Huguenots: Cent ans de persécutions, 1685–1789*. Kindle, 2011.

Joutard, Philippe. "Antoine Court et le désert: La force de l'histoire." *Bulletin de la Société de l'Histoire du Protestantisme Français* (1903–2015) 157 (January–March 2011) 75–81. https://www.jstor.org/stable/24309921.

———. "Identité huguenote, mémoire et histoire, une articulation de longue durée." *Bulletin de la Société de l'Histoire du Protestantisme Français* (1903–2015) 157 (October–December 2011) 621–31. https://www.jstor.org/stable/24310310.

Joxe, Pierre. *L'Édit de Nantes: Réflexions pour un pluralisme religieux*. Paris: Hachette, 2004.

Kelley, Donald R. *The Beginning of Ideology: Consciousness and Society in the French Reformation*. Cambridge: Cambridge University Press, 1981.

Kingdon, Robert M. *Myths about the St. Bartholomew's Day Massacres, 1572–1576*. Cambridge, MA: Harvard University Press, 1988.

Kirschleger, Inès. "'Mon âme est en liberté, et j'ai la paix de la conscience': Résistance et spiritualité des femmes du désert." *Revue d'histoire du protestantisme* 3 (July–December 2018) 569–79. http://www.jstor.org/stable/45142264.

Knecht, R. J. *Renaissance Warrior and Patron, the Reign of Francis I*. Cambridge: Cambridge University Press, 1994.

Krumenacker, Yves. "Les pasteurs français face à la Révolution." *Revue d'histoire du protestantisme* 1 (April–June 2016) 187–206. http://www.jstor.org/stable/44851061.

———. "Marie Durand, une héroïne protestante?" *Clio. Histoire, femmes et sociétés* 30 (2009) 79–98. https://doi.org/10.4000/clio.9389.

Labrousse, Elisabeth. *Une foi, une loi, un roi?" La Révocation de l'Édit de Nantes.* Paris: Payot, 1985.

Lacorne, Denis. *Les frontières de la tolérance.* Paris: Éditions Gallimard, 2016.

La Durand and Daniel Benoît. "Nouveaux échos de la Tour de Constance: Trois lettres inédites de Marie Durand (1752–1759)." *Bulletin de la Société de l'Histoire du Protestantisme Français* (1903–2015) 52 (January–February 1903) 45–59. https://www.jstor.org/stable/24286931.

Lange, Albert de. "Les routes de l'exil des Vaudois du Piémont vers l'Allemagne (1636–1730)." *Diasporas* 20 (2012) 41–57. https://doi.org/10.4000/diasporas.3030.

Leconte, Hubert. *Sur les traces de Vaudois des Alpes au Luberon: Parcours historique.* Avignon: Éditions Cardère, 2003.

Léonard, Émile G. *Le protestant français.* Presses universitaires de France, 1953.

Le Roux, Nicolas. *Le roi, la cour, l'État: De la Renaissance à l'absolutisme.* Seyssel, France: Champ Vallon, 2013.

———. *Les guerres de religion (1559–1629).* Paris: Belin, 2009.

———. *Portraits d'un royaume: Henri III, la noblesse et la Ligue.* Paris: Passés Composés, 2020.

———. *Un régicide au nom de Dieu: L'assassinat d'Henri III. 1er août 1589.* Paris: Gallimard, 2006.

Lévis-Mirepoix, Antoine de. *Les guerres de religion: 1559–1610.* Paris: Librairie Fayard, 1950.

Lindberg, Carter. *The European Reformation.* Oxford: Blackwell, 1996.

Mably, Gabriel Bonnot. "Que l'histoire doit être une école de morale et de politique." In *Chef-d'oeuvre of French Literature,* vol. 1. 237–65. London: Paternoster-Row, 1820.

Machelon, Jean-Pierre. *La laïcité demain: Exclure ou Rassembler?* Paris: CNRS Éditions, 2012.

Mahoney, Irene. *Madame Catherine.* New York: Coward, McCann & Geoghegan, 1975.

Maira, Daniel. "Luther révolutionnaire: Récupération républicaine d'une légende libérale (1814–1848)." *Revue d'histoire du protestantisme* 2 (January–June 2017) 101–17. https://www.jstor.org/stable/44849194.

Marchand, Romain. *Henri de la Tour (1555–1623).* Paris: Éditions Classiques Garnier, 2020.

Marteilhe, Jean. *Mémoires d'un galérien du Roi-Soleil,* edited by André Zysberg. Paris: Éditions Mercure de France, 1989; *The Huguenot Galley Slave.* Miami: Hardpress, 2018.

Martin, A. Lynn. "Papal Policy and the European Conflict, 1559–1572." *The Sixteenth Century Journal,* 11 (1980) 35–48. www.jstor.org/stable/2540031.

Marvick, Elizabeth Wirth. *Louis XIII: The Making of a King.* New Haven: Yale University Press, 1986.

McGrath, Alister E. *A Life of John Calvin.* Oxford: Blackwell, 1990.

———. *Luther's Theology of the Cross: Martin Luther's Theological Breakthrough.* Oxford: Wiley-Blackwell, 1985.

Miquel, Pierre. *Les guerres de religion.* Paris: Fayard, 1980.

Monod, Jean-Claude. *Sécularisation et laïcité.* Paris: Presses universitaires de France, 2007.

Nabonne, Bernard. *Jeanne d'Albret: Reine des Huguenots.* Cressé, France: Éditions des Régionalismes, 2018.

Bibliography

Nelson, Eric. "Remembering the Martyrdom of Saint Francis of Paola: History, Memory and Minim Identity in Seventeenth-Century France." *History and Memory* 26 (2014) 76–105.

Nouveau Petit Robert de la Langue Française, Le. Paris: Le Robert, 2007.

Orcibal, Jean. *Louis XIV et les protestants.* Paris: J.Vrin, 1951.

Pena-Ruiz, Henri. *Qu'est-ce que la laïcité?* Paris: Éditions Gallimard, 2003.

"Peut-on préciser à quel moment les protestants de France commencèrent à être appelés Huguenots?" *Bulletin de la Société de l'Histoire du Protestantisme Français* (1852–1865) 8 (March–May 1859) 122–28. http://www.jstor.org/stable/24282180.

Pouzet, Philippe. "Les origines lyonnaises de la secte des Vaudois." *Revue d'histoire de l'Église de France* 22 (1936) 5-37. https://www.persee.fr/doc/rhef_0300-9505_1936_num_22_94_2757.

Réveillard, Eugène. *La séparation des Églises et de l'État: Précis historique discours et documents.* Paris: Librairie Fischbacher, 1907. https://archive.org/details/lasparationdesoorvuoft.

Roberts, Penny. *Peace and Authority during the French Religious Wars, c.1560-1600.* New York: Palgrave, 2013.

Robespierre, Maximilien. *Œuvres de Maximilien Robespierre.* (July 27, 1793–July 27, 1794). Paris: Presses universitaires de France, 1967. https://archive.org/stream/oeuvrescomplte1orobe#page/ n5/mode/2up.

Sagnier, Charles. *La tour de Constance et ses prisonnières.* Nîmes: C. Lacour, 1996.

Schaeffer, Adolph. *Les Huguenots du seizième siècle.* Paris: Grassart, 1870.

Soppelsa, Jacques. "De la laïcité." *Revue Politique et Parlementaire* 1038 (January–March 2006) 2–5.

Stéphan, Raoul. *L'Épopée huguenote.* Paris: La Colombe, 1945.

Sutherland, N. M. "The Assassination of François Duc De Guise, February 1563." *The Historical Journal* 24 (June 1981) 279–95. http://www.jstor.org/stable/2638787.

———. *The Massacre of St. Bartholomew and the European conflict, 1559-1572.* New York: Barnes & Noble, 1973.

Treasure, Geoffrey. *The Huguenots.* New Haven, CT: Yale University Press, 2014.

Vovelle, Michel. *La Révolution française:1789-1799.* Paris: Armand Colin, 2006.

Walker, Williston, et al. *A History of the Christian Church.* 4th ed. New York: Charles Scribner's Sons, 1985.

Walsby, Malcolm. *L'imprimé en Europe occidental, 1470-1680.* Rennes: Presses universitaires de Rennes, 2020.

Wanegffelen, Thierry. *L'édit de Nantes: Une histoire européenne de la tolérance du XVIe au XXe siècle.* Paris: Librairie générale française, 1998.

Whelan, Ruth. "Enfin Libres!" *Société de l'histoire du protestantisme français* (1903–2015) 161 (April–June 2015) 285–93. https://www.jstor.org/stable/44475201.

Willaime, Jean-Paul. "L'expression des religions, une chance pour la démocratie." *Revue Projet* 342 (2014) 5–14. https://www.cairn.info/revue-projet-2014-5-page-5.htm.

Zeghal, Malika. "La constitution du Conseil Français du Culte Musulman: Reconnaissance politique d'un Islam français?" *Archives de sciences sociales des religions* 129 (January–March 2005) 1–14.

Zuber, Roger. "Les psaumes dans l'histoire des Huguenots." *Bulletin de la Société de l'Histoire du Protestantisme Français* (1903-2015) 123 (July–September 1977) 350–61.

Index

Index

Index

Index

INDEX

Printed in Great Britain
by Amazon